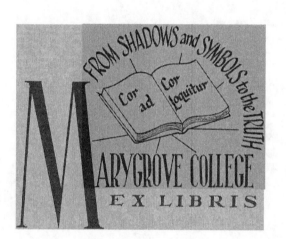

JOSEF PIEPER

THE SILENCE OF
ST. THOMAS

Three Essays

TRANSLATED BY
JOHN MURRAY, S.J.
AND
DANIEL O'CONNOR

PANTHEON

Contents

I

On Thomas Aquinas

II

The Negative Element in the Philosophy of St. Thomas Aquinas

III

The Timeliness of Thomism

I

ON THOMAS AQUINAS

His Life and Work

A chance perusal of any of Augustine's writings,
even a page from his most abstract work, *On the
Trinity*, will convey the unmistakable impression:
this was thought and written by a man of flesh and
blood. But let someone take a similar glimpse into
the tight structure of the *Summa Theologica* of St.
Thomas Aquinas, and he will be tempted to ask:
Were these sentences really set down by a living
man or did not rather the objective content formulate itself undisturbed—neither blurred nor warmed
—by the breath of a living thinker? The vital prod-
ucts of Augustine's thinking never allow us to forget their source in his personal life, from which
they spring forth like the blossom from its root and
stem. But the language of St. Thomas suggests its
origin in a living mind as little as crystal suggests
the essential liquid from which it is formed.

Yet only on a superficial interpretation would
one infer from the untroubled and unhurried seren-
ity of the work that the author himself lived in
freedom from outer or inner disturbances. On the

other hand, it is certainly clear that the *Summa Theologica* can only be the work of a heart fundamentally at peace. St. Thomas did not discover and map out his majestic outline of Christian teaching in the "silence of the cloister cell." It was not in some idyllic sphere of retirement cut off from the happenings in the world that he lived out his life. Such presentations, as untrue to history as they are impermissibly simplified, not only color, or rather *dis*color in many particulars the conventional portraits of Thomas; they frequently have an effect on biographical studies which make higher claims to accuracy.

The very fact that a work of such unperturbed objectivity and such deep, radiating peace could grow from a life which, far from being untroubled, consumed itself in strife, gives us an insight into the special quality of the man. His work, incidentally, shows immediate reflection and evidence of an outspokenly combative cast of mind, which, however, even in the heat of battle, was never divorced from the norms of truth and love and consequently never lost its fundamental peace. The writing *On the Perfection of the Spiritual Life*, originating in his forty-fifth year, ends with the following words: "If anyone wishes to write against this, I will welcome it. For true and false will in no better way be revealed and uncovered than in resistance to a contradiction, according to the saying: 'Iron is sharpened by iron.' (Prov. 27:17). And between us and them may God judge, Who is blessed in eternity. Amen."

Count Landulf of Aquino, Lord of Loretto and Belcastro, was one of the most loyal vassals of the Hohenstaufen Emperor Frederick II. During the years of the sharpest struggle between Emperor and Pope his youngest son Thomas was preparing himself for an office both remote and superior to the conflict—the priestly office of preaching the truth. He was studying at the Benedictine Abbey of Monte Cassino which at that time also served as an imperial castle, situated on the border between Hohenstaufen and papal territory. Under these circumstances, Thomas could hardly expect a secure life sheltered from external disturbances and dangers.

In the first months of the year 1239, when Frederick II was excommunicated, Monte Cassino came directly into the zone of battle. The garrison of the castle, half of which had to be supported by the abbey, was more than doubled. The fortifications were expanded by order of the Emperor himself, who had first entered his Sicilian kingdom twenty years previously at this very spot. In this same year, the monks had to leave their monastery.

Among their company was the fifteen-year-old Thomas Aquinas.

This exodus led the boy to Naples—to the beginning of his particular destiny; it took him permanently out of seclusion and thrust him into the heated center of all the intellectual battles of that time. The University of Naples, founded in the year of Thomas's birth, was the first "pure state university,"—not a "school for seminarians but a school for imperial officials."[1] Frederick II had designed it to work against the Church. Here, according to custom, Thomas studied the "liberal arts." What is most important is that, under the tutelage of the Irishman, Peter of Hibernia, he became acquainted with the writings of Aristotle, which were at that time extremely suspect in the Church. "Aristotelian!" was an abusive epithet in the mouths of the orthodox, comparable to nihilist, freethinker, man of the "Enlightenment." It was in Naples, too, that the flame of that urban "youth movement," which was filling the ranks of the first generation of the mendicant orders, was first kindled in the heart of the young nobleman.

These two words, "Aristotle" and "mendicants," indicate the two most important disputes which in the first half of the thirteenth century rocked Christendom with a passionate violence we can

scarcely understand. Both Aristotle and the mendicant orders stood in the midst of a storm of ap-
provals and rejections. At the time when Thomas
came to Naples, hardly a decade and a half after the
death of St. Francis of Assisi (1226), the two
mendicant orders had not yet achieved any general
recognition. On the contrary, all papal recognitions
and privileges could not prevent the representatives
of the established society—the temporal lords, the
rising, urban middle class and the secular clergy—
from calling these remarkable new "poor men"
"demented" (which was partly understandable),
and even "heretical" or "sons of the Anti-Christ."
This, of course, did not stem the upsurge of the
young spiritual movement, nourished as it was by
so many sources, among them the fundamental historical impulse of the times.

Above all it attracted, as if they were its rightful
portion, young men of noble birth. We also know
that both the Franciscan and the Dominican con-
vents in Paris received many recruits from the student body. The records are similar for the University of Bologna, and quite probably the same
was true of the University of Frederick II at
Naples. For all these young men, events such as the
following must have been like the illumination of
sudden lightning and a charm to capture their
hearts: In the year 1231, a professor at the Uni-

7

versity of Paris, Jean of St. Giles, was delivering a lecture on evangelical poverty in the Dominican Priory of St. Jacques. As he spoke, he was so carried away by his subject that he broke off his lecture and begged the Prior for the habit. Then, himself become a Dominican, he went on to finish his lecture. One could consider this report legendary, were it not a fact that in this very way the Dominicans acquired a chair, their second, at the University of Paris—a chair which Thomas Aquinas was to occupy twenty years later.

The power inherent in all these new things drew the young liberal arts student irresistibly into the discussions and forced him to a decision. At the age of twenty, Thomas entered the Order of St. Dominic which combines the ideal of poverty with that of study.

In more than one way this decision must have been a provocation to Frederick II, since Thomas was the son of one of his vassals. And it is probable that to Count Landulf of Aquino—whose brother was abbot of powerful Monte Cassino, and who doubtless preferred to think of his son rather as a successor to this almost princely office than as a mendicant friar—the whole mendicant order movement must have appeared as something positively inferior and disreputable, a judgment in which his whole family was likely to concur.

8

And though it would be absurd to seek in Thomas's decision motives of politics, even ecclesiastical politics (the young man had already glimpsed the superiority of truth over worldly power), in the distorting mirror of minds dominated by power politics his entrance into a mendicant order might easily have been construed as a decision against the Emperor and for the Pope, as whose particular friends and tools the new communities of Franciscans and Dominicans were regarded. Accordingly, the haste with which the Friars Preachers sped Thomas out of the imperial district and away from his family is thoroughly understandable. They sent him forthwith on the way toward Paris.

But Thomas did not arrive so easily at the place of his future fame. On the way he was captured by his brothers and held prisoner. There are many indications that this was not done without the consent or even the assistance of the Emperor himself. In any case, Pope Innocent IV protested unsuccessfully to the Emperor against this act of violence. Thomas was imprisoned in his father's castle of San Giovanni for over a year until, with the aid of his sister, he finally succeeded in making his escape.

He resumed immediately the interrupted journey to Paris. It is noteworthy that Thomas's traveling companion, Johannes Teutonicus, then Master

General of the order, and later his teacher, Albert
the Great, were both Germans. Johannes Teutonicus was a Westphalian from the ecclesiastical district around Münster. In this same year 1245, when
Thomas moved on to France, a General Council
was being assembled at Lyons, which dethroned
the Emperor and disinherited his line. While this
threatening storm brewed in the West, Thomas ar-
rived in Paris, a city so eminently the metropolis of
theological studies that Scholastic research could
claim that in the entire medieval era no *Summa
Theologica* was written which does not relate to
the university near Notre Dame Cathedral.

Thomas found the Friars Preachers of St. Jacques
Priory in a precarious situation. They, as well as the
Franciscans, could hardly show themselves in the
streets without being insulted or attacked. The
King of France, Saint Louis (later to become a
friend of St. Thomas, who was some ten years his
junior) had found it necessary to detail a royal
guard to the convent to protect it against assault. In
the whole order, special prayers were prescribed
begging God to put an end to this evil, which was
everywhere rampant, but particularly acute in Paris.

Thomas, then only a little over twenty, and because of his strength, his slow movements and his
characteristic silence, dubbed by his fellow students
"the dumb ox," probably did not suffer unduly

from these circumstances; though, of course, they do not convey the idyllic picture of a peaceful cloister cell.

An event of quite another sort must have claimed his entire attention: In the year of Thomas's arrival, Albertus Magnus began to teach in Paris. The friendship that developed out of this encounter of master and pupil and the fruitfulness of their common work were to change the intellectual face of the West. A few years after their first meeting, in 1248, the year in which the foundation stone of Cologne Cathedral was laid, both Albert and Thomas were transferred to Cologne. Albert was instructed to establish there a college for the Friars Preachers. For Thomas, these years held the gift of fruitful silence and intellectual ripening. The halfway mark of his stay in Cologne coincided with the halfway mark of the century; for Thomas, it was already the halfway mark of his life.

The years in Cologne were ended by a letter from the Master General, Johannes Teutonicus, in which Thomas was summoned to prepare himself for a teaching assignment which led him back to Paris. Meanwhile, at the University of Paris, the old battle between the secular clergy and the mendicants had burst into new flame. It was now a battle between points of teaching as well as for teaching chairs. And it was a battle not always honorably waged. The headstrong defenders of the traditional forces, led by the pugnacious William of St. Amour, made use of very questionable weapons. Lies, calumny, falsification, and slander were by no means uncommon. But on the other hand it is also reported that the Dominican scholars terrorized the professors of the secular clergy and even the rector of the university with their pressure tactics. This was the whirlpool into which Thomas was returning.

A new personal contact awaited him, with the Franciscan Bonaventure. It is true that the old annals make scant mention of a friendship between these two saintly teachers of Christendom. Yet there is a compelling truth in the thought that these two great ones, above the feuds of their followers, were linked in friendship. Thomas and Bonaventure, who had entered their respective orders in the same year, found themselves at that time in the same trying situation. Both men, as mendicants, had been refused permission to begin an independent teaching course at the university. As the result of an explicit papal order, both were finally granted permission on the same day.

It seemed at first that, for Thomas, the permission alone would not be enough, for the University boycotted his inaugural lecture. And later on, dur-

ing one of his lectures, an official of the philosophical faculty and a follower of William of St. Amour
(who had meanwhile been banished), got up and
loudly recited a poem lampooning the mendicants.
Still, such happenings could not prevent Thomas
from becoming one of the most beloved and celebrated teachers at the Paris university.

In these stormy early years of his first teaching
assignment, Thomas composed his first work, *On
Essence and Existence*, a work with the sharp clarity of a mountain panorama. The noisy and dis-
graceful tempest of strife and jealousy in which he
had to work had not been able to cloud the mirror
of a single sentence. The earliest, almost contemporary, biography of Thomas, which was written
by William of Tocco, Prior at Benevento, mentions
repeatedly his enormous power of concentration.
While he was writing the *Summa Contra Gentiles*, it
frequently seemed as if his senses were numbed.
Once, while dictating at night, he did not notice
that the candle he was holding had burned down
and singed his fingers.

The *Summa Contra Gentiles*, which in spite of
its title is anything but a polemical work, was written in Italy. After he had taught three years as full
professor of theology at the University of Paris,
Thomas was called to the papal court, often lo-
cated in those days at Viterbo or Orvieto. From

then until his death, Thomas never remained
longer than two or three years in the same place or
in the same office. He taught three years at the court
of Urban IV. After that he went to Rome for two
years, with the assignment to establish there a college for his order. At this time he conceived the
outline and began working on the first part of the
Summa Theologica, his enormous main work, on
which he labored for seven years, without finishing
it entirely. After these two years in Rome, a new
pope, Clement IV, called him once again to the
papal court at Viterbo. The attempt, previously
made, to appoint the mendicant friar Archbishop of
Naples had been frustrated by his own resistance,
even though he had been canonically designated.[2] In
Viterbo, Thomas again stayed only two years.
Those were the years in which the tragedy of the
last of the Hohenstaufens, the boy Konradin, was
consummated. At that time, Thomas wrote his
treatise *On the Governance of Princes*, which contains, among other things, the magnificent chapter
on the reward of kings.

That, in 1263, the former professor of the University of Paris should be called back for a second
time to Paris at the direction of his order was
against all custom in the thirteenth century. However, a man of his intellectual powers, and perhaps,

too, a man of his unshakable calm, was evidently
urgently needed at the university. Thomas, for the
third time, took the road to Paris. (Here it may be
noted that, as a mendicant friar, Thomas made all
these journeys on foot—unless he had to take a ship
to cross the waters—in much the same way as his
teacher, Albert, who walked through nearly the
whole of Europe during his long life, earning
thereby his nickname "the Boot.")

The returning teacher was awaited not by one
opposing faction, but by three. The battle against
the mendicants had ceased to center around teaching chairs; instead, the attacks were now directed
against the theological and religious principles of
the orders. The two additional factions, both
aroused by the key word "Aristotle," were so-
called Augustinianism and Latin Averroism. We
shall have occasion to treat of these two opposing
theories and the conflicts they aroused.

It appears that Thomas belonged to that race of
men whose imposing calm grows in proportion to
the noise and tumult around them. "We never
knew him to lose his composure," remarked one of
his confrères who had long lived in the same priory
with him. At all events, the productivity of these
years in Paris—once again it was only a three-year
period—passes understanding. In this brief, em-
battled period Thomas wrote, in addition to short

polemic pamphlets, voluminous commentaries on nearly all the major works of Aristotle and on all the epistles of St. Paul as well as the gospel of St. John. He produced the great *Quaestiones Dispu-tatae* on the virtues, and, as a short summary of the whole of theology, the *Compendium Theologiae*. Finally, he wrote numerous treatises for the *Summa Theologica*. In these works Thomas did not with-draw from the intellectual conflict. Rather, the works listed are for the most part contributions to it. And when, in 1272, his superiors recalled him from Paris (apparently on a sudden decision), their main intention was to cool the heat of that conflict. In any case, his successor in the teaching chair in-clined more strongly toward the Augustinian, i.e., the traditional direction. It also deserves to be men-tioned that among the students of St. Thomas at Paris was a Florentine Dominican, Remigio de' Girolami, who in later years was to become the teacher of his fellow-citizen, Dante.

Thomas was once more commissioned to found a college for the order, this time at the place of his first decision: Naples. But in the year after, the Pope summoned him to a new General Council at Lyons. Toward the end of the winter 1273-74, Thomas set out on the long journey whose goal he did not reach. On the way, in the Cistercian monas-tery of Fossanova, he fell mortally ill and a short time later died, not quite fifty years old. Later in the same year, Bonaventure also died, at the very council to which both men had been called.

At the canonization process, the abbot of Fossanova testified under oath that the community had not celebrated the Mass of the Dead at the funeral of St. Thomas but, instead, the Mass *Os Justi*, in honor of a holy confessor, the Introit of which begins with the words: "The mouth of the just man shall meditate wisdom and his tongue shall speak judgment: the law of his God is in his heart."

His Personality

It has been said that the work of St. Thomas is the most impersonal of the entire thirteenth century. It is true that, in the thirty volumes of his *Opera Omnia*, there is hardly a single immediately personal trait to discover—unless we consider this very absence as a mirror of his personality. It is doubtless an accident, though a significant one, that only one letter of St. Thomas has come down to us—the letter he wrote, shortly before his death, to the abbot of Monte Cassino. This single letter, however, deals with a textual difficulty in Gregory's Commentary on Job and is too much an expression of expert opinion to afford the opportunity —as Goethe puts it—"of preserving the immediacy (*das Unmittelbare*) of living existence" and revealing it to us.

Those, however, who knew Thomas personally, must have sensed from his immediate presence the qualities of saintliness. And he must have been singularly impressive—a man of tall and erect bearing, at once strong and sensitive; with a mighty and commanding forehead, his skin gleaming like golden wheat, his face shining with a radiance that was never extinguished. There could be no doubting the special holiness of this friar, who frequently could be seen pacing up and down the convent halls in great strides, head erect, alone, meditating. The witnesses at the canonization process, many of whom had long been associated with Thomas, had nothing to report concerning unusual ascetic exercises or mortifications. But they testified that Thomas loved peace; that he was sparing regarding himself, humble, and full of goodness for his fellows. He was a lover of poverty and his heart was entirely directed toward the divine.

One particular trait was named most frequently by the more than thirty witnesses, and often in first place: *Castitas*. St. Thomas must have been a man of such purity and radiance of character that everyone coming into his presence seemed to feel something like a fresh, cool breeze.

When Thomas was held prisoner in the isolation of the castle of San Giovanni, his brothers had tried in various ways to turn him from his decision to become a mendicant friar. (Reginald, one of the two brothers who had imprisoned him, was a poet of some note in his own day, known in particular for love poems in the vernacular. A Swedish scholar edited these poems during the first World War.)[3] One day the brothers sent a practiced courtesan into Thomas's chamber. We know only that he turned her out roughly. However, it seems that the twenty-year-old lad went in those few moments through a terrifying interior struggle. William of Tocco writes: Thomas immediately thereafter collapsed at the threshold of his chamber and fell exhausted into a deep sleep out of which he awoke with a loud scream. The scream was caused by an exceedingly painful operation. An angel had girded him tightly with a cincture in order to make him inviolable against all future temptation to impurity. Toward the end of his life Thomas related all of this to his friend and secretary, Reginald of Piperno.

Since we nowadays think that all a man needs for acquisition of truth is to exert his brain more or less vigorously, and since we consider an *ascetic* approach to knowledge hardly sensible, we have lost the awareness of the close bond that links the knowing of truth to the condition of purity. Thomas says that unchastity's first-born daughter is blindness of the spirit.[4] Only he who wants nothing for himself, who is not subjectively "interested," can know the truth. On the other hand, an impure, selfishly corrupted will-to-pleasure destroys both resoluteness of spirit and the ability of the psyche to listen in silent attention to the language of reality.

To perceive this language, i.e., to grasp the truth of real things—this is the true passion of St. Thomas. This fundamental character trait leads us to an understanding of his astonishing courage and his no less astonishing humility. When Thomas, for instance, ranged himself on the side of the pagan Aristotle against the traditional philosophico-theological trends (an undertaking requiring great boldness), he did this not from a spirit of opposition to traditional doctrines or from a mania for innovations, but rather because his intrepid approach to truth recognized the voice of reality in Aristotle's work. This same intrepidity made him ask, in his *Commentary on the Book of Job*, whether Job's bold conversation with the Lord God did not violate reverence—to which he gave the almost outrageous answer: truth does not change according to the standing of the person to whom it is addressed; he who speaks truthfully is invulnerable, no matter who may be his adversary.[5]

Another facet of this courage is shown in an incident pertaining to his last years in Paris—a time when the eyes of all Europe were fixed on him. At a public and formal disputation of some controversial points of his teaching, Thomas, after calmly presenting his arguments, had no hesitation to submit them for the final decision to the Bishop of Paris and the university faculty. (Many years later, the fiery Franciscan John Peckham, become Archbishop of Canterbury, who was Thomas's opponent in the dispute, recalled the incident with great admiration.) If Thomas, at the height of his fame as a teacher, was capable of such humility, we have to see in it not so much the sign of modest self-effacement, but rather the courage to face truth, to which belongs the courage to see in a thesis neither less nor more than its premises warrant. This tranquil courage, neither afraid of rejection nor overly eager for approval, shows that Thomas was happily free of all self-importance. We have a prayer he wrote in which he asks God to let him be cheerful without falling into frivolity, and become mature without falling into pompousness.

We have become used to see in an intellectual

dispute something in the nature of a fencing match, or at least of a contest with victors and vanquished. And by and large such disputes are carried on according to the rules of such contests. Thomas would have thought it unbearably self-important had anyone spoken of his "victory" over Averroes or Siger of Brabant. For him, an intellectual dispute was a common striving for the victory, not of one of the contenders, but of truth. Even the erring party, he says, is meritorious; for error, too, may serve to illuminate truth.[6] Accordingly, in his disputes with opponents of contrary positions, Thomas violates all fighting codes. He challenges the opponent not at the weakest spot in his position—too cheap a procedure for Thomas, who was noble in more than name—but, rather, he meets him precisely in the area of his strongest arguments. Often enough Thomas is the first to bring the actual force of these arguments to light; frequently, it is through his formulations that the objections of his adversaries gain in persuasive power. Thus, in the study of such a work as the *Summa Contra Gentiles*, it is an exhilarating experience to see an intrepid mind meet the essential questions squarely, with no attempt at side-stepping them.

One cannot touch on the theme "Thomas and the truth" and remain silent about the devotion with which he was the *teacher* of truth. To lead a man from error to truth—this he considered the greatest service which one man can render another.[7] And nothing characterized Thomas the teacher so strongly as his prayer and hope that his life would not outlast his teaching. Once he could no longer teach, then life itself might as well be taken away from him. Teaching, for Thomas, is something other and greater than to impart by one method or another the "findings of research"; something other and greater than the report of a thinker on the results of his inquiry, not to mention the ways and by-ways of his search. Teaching is a process that goes on between living men. The teacher looks not only at the truth of things; at the same time he looks at the faces of living men who desire to know this truth. Love of truth and love of men—only the two together constitute a teacher. No small part of the whole work of St. Thomas was written in answer to requests of friends—sometimes the request of a prince, or, just as often, the request of a nobody. Once a young confrère from Venice, a "beginner," submitted to him no less than thirty-six separate questions, which were not even clearly formulated, and requested an answer within four days. Thomas, who could legitimately have excused himself with the excessive demands made on him by more important work, not only supplied the answers but also formulated the questions more precisely; and in addition to that, he met the requested time limit.

Teaching demands above all else the capacity of survey and of simplification, and the ability and effort to think from the premise of a beginner. This capacity of true simplification St. Thomas possessed to a high degree, and he bent every effort to take his student's point of view as a premise. The best energies and the best part of his life he devoted not to a work of "research" but to a textbook for beginners, which is nonetheless the result of the deepest immersion into truth. The *Summa Theologica* is expressly written *ad eruditionem incipientium*, for the instruction of beginners, as it is plainly stated several times in the preface. In this preface Thomas mentions the boredom produced by the over-familiar, and the confusion experienced by beginners through the excesses of misplaced scholarship. The teaching method of St. Thomas, contemporaries report, fascinated his students precisely through its freshness and originality. To quote Martin Grabmann, Thomas was the first to eliminate the underbrush of "scholastic" hair-splitting, which had already become traditional in the thirteenth century—to be revived, it is true, in new profusion by the late Scholastics.

What astounding capacities of survey and simplification are revealed in the threefold division of the *Summa Theologica:* "In the first part we will treat of God, in the second, of the turning back of spirit-endowed creatures to God, in the third of Christ, Who is in His Humanity the Way on which we will succeed to God."[8] What power of simplification in a sentence such as the following, which embraces a *"summa"* of Christian teaching on life: "Three kinds of knowledge are necessary to man for his salvation: the knowledge of what he must believe, the knowledge of that for which he must pray, and the knowledge of what he must do. The first is taught in the creeds of our Faith, the second in the prayer of the Lord, the third in the commandments."[9]

The intimate fusion, in this towering mind, of the innate gift for probing, grasping, and illuminating reality to its depth, and the capacity for giving it inspired and convincing form as a teacher, becomes overwhelmingly evident in the tersely formulated eleventh chapter in the fourth book of the *Summa Contra Gentiles.* In this chapter, that stands perhaps unmatched even in Thomas's own work, he undertakes to describe the ordered structure of total reality, building it up from stone to angel and to God Himself, in a truly ravishing range of vision. This is what it says:

Where things differ in nature, we find different modes of emanation. The more this emanation takes place in the innermost reality of a thing, the higher is its order of being. Now, of all things, the inanimate take the lowest place and from them no emanation is possible except by the action of one on another . . .

The next higher order after inanimate bodies is formed by the plants whose emanation proceeds from within inasmuch as the plant's inner juice is converted into seed, which being committed to the soil grows into a new plant. Accordingly, we find here the first traces of life, since living things are those which move themselves into activity. Nevertheless, the plant's life is still imperfect, for although its emanation proceeds from within, that which emanates emerges out of it and is ultimately entirely outside it. Thus, from the juice of the tree, first the blossom is produced and then the fruit which, although still connected with the tree, is outside its bark. When the fruit is ripe it separates itself entirely from the tree, falls to the earth, and brings forth out of its own seminal force a new plant. Indeed, if we consider the matter carefully we shall see that the first principle of this emanation is something extraneous, for the inner juice of the tree is sucked up by the roots from the earth, whence the plant draws its nourishment.

Above the level of plant life is a higher level, that of the sensitive soul, the proper emanation whereof, though beginning from without, terminates within. Also, the further the emanation proceeds, the more

does it penetrate within, for the sensible object im-
presses a form on the external senses, whence it passes
to the imagination and, further still, to the storehouse
of the memory. Yet in every process of this kind of
emanation, the beginning and the end are in different
subjects, for no sensitive power reflects on itself.
Therefore, this degree of life transcends that of plants
insomuch as it is more intimate; and yet it is not a perfect life, since the emanation is always from one thing
to another. The highest degree of life, therefore, is that
which is according to intellect, for the intellect reflects
on itself and can understand itself. There are, however,
in the intellectual life several levels to be distinguished.
The human intellect, although it is capable of knowing
itself, still takes the beginning of its knowledge from
without. Man is not able to know without a sense image. More perfect is the life of the angel, whose knowing spirit does not acquire self-knowledge from without, but rather knows itself through itself. Even so, life
has still not reached its last and highest step, because
the angel's spiritual image of itself, although wholly
within it, is still not one with its being. For in the
angel, to know and to be are not the same thing. The
highest perfection of life belongs to God, Whose understanding is not distinguished from His Being.

For its true effect, this sovereignly constructed
passage should be *heard* in the Latin. The language
of St. Thomas does not have the quality of beauty

proper to a work of art, as we find it, for instance, in Augustine; it is beautiful as a perfect instrument is beautiful. And yet, there are in the writings of St. Thomas numerous chapters whose sentences move in such rhythmic cadence toward their *conclusio,* their final "therefore," that one can think of no more fitting comparison than that with the determined stride of the final measures in an organ fugue by Johann Sebastian Bach. It would be strange indeed if, as a shallow judgment of the humanists has decreed, the secret of language should have been barred to the very man who gave Christendom the hymn: *Adoro Te devote, Latens Deitas.*

His Conception of the World

We have already mentioned the two opposing theories at the University of Paris against whom Thomas had to defend his own positions on God and the world. They were, firstly, the traditional and predominating trends, primarily philosophical but also theological, which we are accustomed to designate as Augustinianism; and secondly, Latin Averroism. From the viewpoint of these two opposing theories we have, perhaps, the best opportunity of making clear the unique character of St. Thomas's teaching.

In the strife between Thomas Aquinas and medieval Augustinianism two of the most revealing points in dispute were the following. Thomas taught the unity of the substantial form, while Augustinianism accepted *several* form-giving principles in man. Thomas asserted that all our knowledge, including the spiritual, and also our knowledge of God, took its starting point (and therefore always remained somehow dependent upon) sense perception,[10] while Augustinianism claimed that spiritual knowledge was independent of sense perception. At first sight, this appears to be a petty quarrel between "schools." But for Thomas it involved nothing less than the saving of creation as a visible reality from any attempt at reduction, devaluation, or sheer annihilation.

What is the meaning of these two theses of St. Thomas? They mean that in man there is not one part—the soul—which is the "real" man, and another part—the body, a separate reality—which is the instrument or even the prison of the soul; rather, body and soul are an immediate existential unity. And further, that the "real" man is not the soul alone but precisely this existential unity of body and soul. The body belongs to the essence of man.[11] The second thesis means that it is not the spiritual soul which is the ultimate bearer of our knowledge, but *man*—composed of body and soul. Therefore, our knowledge is always an image of our own being; knowledge is, like our being itself, an indissoluble unity of spiritual and corporal (sentient) principles.

These theses mean more than they directly express. In them is mirrored, as we have already remarked, that affirmation of the natural reality of creation which is so characteristic of St. Thomas: All created things are good because they were created by God. For the same reason, they have a reality and effectiveness of their own, which may not be ignored or obliterated through making absolute in one way or another the "spiritual" or "religious" element in man. Moreover, the reality of creation in man, the natural light of his reason, his five senses, all the powers of his being, have their place and assignment in the make-up of man *as Christian*. (On the other hand, one may well say of St. Augustine, without violating the reverence due to this great saint and great thinker, that, as the history of Christian teaching shows, his work falls more easily into the danger of being construed or, rather, *mis*construed in the sense of a de-actualization and devaluation of the visible reality of creation.) Of course, Thomas is also aware of the injury caused to creation through original sin. In fact, he even says that the more deeply a man recognizes the true being of created things, the more this knowledge becomes for him a source of sadness—because out of every created reality can arise a menace to salvation.[12] But Thomas also knows that the same Christ Who founded the New Creation is simultaneously the eternal archetype of the first creation.[13]

In his *Commentary on St. John's Epistle*,[14] St. Thomas remarks that we can find in Sacred Scripture three different meanings for the term "the world": first, "the world" as the creation of God, and second, as the creation perfected in Christ; last, as the material perversion of the order of creation. To "the world" in this last-named sense, and to this world only, may one apply the saying of St. John: "The world is seated in wickedness" (1 John 5:19). It is precisely the claim of St. Thomas that the first meaning of "world" (as creation) may not be identified nor interchanged with the third—("world" as material perversion of the order of creation); the world as creation is *not* seated in wickedness.

A single common denominator underlies all these theses. To affirm and accept the reality of creation in all its provinces is the response befitting quite particularly the Christian. This is the key to understanding his thesis on the unity of the substantial form in man. This is likewise the foundation of St. Thomas's teaching on the true place of natural reason and philosophy with regard to supernatural faith and theology. From the standpoint of his affirmation of the wholeness of creation, one may, perhaps, also understand the ease with which, in the *Summa Theologica,* he recommends bathing and sleeping as remedies against melancholy of the soul.[15]

One of the most penetrating remarks in Chesterton's book on St. Thomas is the following: If, conformable to Carmelite custom, a fitting epithet such as John "of the Cross" or Thérèse "of the Child Jesus" were sought for Thomas Aquinas, the one most appropriate would be "Thomas of the Creator," *Thomas a Creatore.*

Only when we have truly recognized that the intention of St. Thomas is always directed toward God the Creator and His creation are we competent to evaluate his "Aristotelianism." Aristotle is for St. Thomas (in the measure in which he follows him) nothing more nor less than a clear mirror of the natural reality of creation, a great and rich mind in which the *ordo* of the natural universe was inscribed.[16] Thomas confronted the work of Aristotle with greater freedom and independence than is normally the case in the attitude of a school toward the work of its master—the "Thomistic" school not excepted.

It is also not correct to speak of a "Hellenizing" of Christian doctrine in the teaching of St. Thomas. When the Reformers of the sixteenth century attempted to "purge" Christian theology of the supposedly Hellenizing scholastic element, it became quickly evident (and in the properly "reformed" theology of Karl Barth, for example, it is still evident today) that they were risking the error of removing from the Christian consciousness the reality of creation itself. (It is an unhistorical legend that Luther burned the *Summa Theologica* along with the papal bull in the marketplace at Wittenberg. The true story of that incident, however, makes a more telling point. A recently uncovered report of that auto-da-fé testifies that there was the intention of burning the *Summa* along with the papal document, but no one could be found who was willing to part with his copy!)

Far from being or signifying a secularization of genuine Christian teaching, the affirmation of the reality of creation in the theology of St. Thomas surges from the very depths of Christian intuition, namely, from reverence for the reality of the Incarnation of God. According to St. Thomas, the Evangelist John had deliberately said the Word was made *flesh*, in order to exclude the Manichaean principle that the body is evil.[17]

It is this altogether religious and theological root which differentiates St. Thomas's openness to the world from the truly secularizing concepts of his second and more dangerous opponent—Latin Averroism, named after Averroes (1126-1198), one of the great Arabian commentators on Aristotle. We are not concerned here with the individual points of teaching (the numerical unity of the intellect in all men, the eternity of the world, the denial of free will). The decisive point is that Averroism radically severed the connection between faith and reason, between theology and philosophy. It maintained the complete independence of philosophical thinking from faith and theology. Moreover, it overvalued excessively this separated philosophical thinking,[18] inasmuch as it expected to find in it the true and final wisdom, i.e., an answer which would satisfy the human spirit inquiring into the meaning of the world and human life. To this, Thomas says: The Christian can neither seek nor find a wisdom outside Christ.[19] A single divine grace exceeds, in its existential value, the whole of the natural universe.[20]

One notices that by this decisive secularization of thought, Latin Averroism is fundamentally the forerunner of the Renaissance and, therefore, of modern philosophy and science in general.

This family likeness extends to another, rarely

noticed characteristic. In Latin Averroism appeared, for the first time, the purely historical approach to the interpretation of philosophy—the opinion that the true object of philosophy is its own history. For Siger of Brabant, the leader of the Averroists at the University of Paris, the study of philosophy signifies the exploration of the historical systems of philosophy, irrespective of whether they were true or false.[21] Here for the first time appears that modern type of philosopher who, instead of discussing his true subject, reality, discusses something quite different, the philosophies. A magnificent and invigorating retort given by Thomas to Siger of Brabant should preface all translations and interpretations of Thomas, in order to cut short from the very start any attempt to take the "Universal Teacher" of the Church himself as a merely "historical" phenomenon: "The study of philosophy does not mean to learn what others have thought but to learn what is the truth of things."[22]

In spite of this unequivocal opposition and in spite of the enormous differences between Thomas and Averroism, it is apparently Thomas's destiny to be confused with his secularized opponent. Three years after the death of St. Thomas, for example, several misinterpreted propositions from his writings were condemned by the Bishop of Paris and enumerated on the same list with the errors of Averroism.

Since that time, not only has Thomas been canonized by the Church; he is also the first man, as Martin Grabmann says, to be canonized *qua* theologian and teacher. Moreover, Thomas has been solemnly declared a Doctor of the Church—and, indeed, the "Universal Doctor of the Church." Pius XI says of him that the Church testifies in every way that she has made his teaching her own.[23] Yet the censure that his teaching is tainted with a virtually pagan worldliness has persisted since the days when William of St. Amour wrote against Albert and his great pupil: "They arrogate divine wisdom to themselves, although they are more familiar with worldly wisdom." To which Thomas answered: "The opinion of those who say with regard to the truth of faith that it is a matter of complete indifference what one thinks about creation, provided one has a true interpretation of God . . . . is notoriously false. For an error about creation is reflected in a false opinion about God."[24]

This censure is likely to take the following forms: the confidence which St. Thomas puts in natural reason goes beyond the Christian norm; his philosophy and theology are much too rational, indeed too rationalistic;[25] they have a tendency to offer facile, all-inclusive "solutions" to all questions;

the harsh daylight of his syllogisms deprives the human spirit of the dark glow of the mysteries of our faith; the element of mystery in supernatural truth is almost totally suppressed in favor of its supposedly demonstrable rationality . . . and so on.

It is indisputably true that a great number of "neo-scholastic" or "Thomistic" presentations, "according to the teaching of St. Thomas," provide real cause and seeming justification for such objections. Thomas himself, however, goes so far in the recognition of mystery, both in creation and in God, that for us modern Christians, who seldom hear about the incomprehensibility of God, it comes as a cause of alarm when we find our ignorance so intrepidly and clearly pointed out in the *Summa Theologica*. For in this "summary" of his teaching on God, Thomas begins by saying: "Because we are not capable of knowing what God is but only what He is not, we cannot contemplate how God is but only how He is not."[26] Evidently, Thomas did not wish to withhold this basic thought of "negative" theology even from the beginner. And in the *Quaestiones Disputatae* is even said: "*Hoc est ultimum cognitionis humanae de Deo; quod sciat se Deum nescire*, this is the ultimate in human knowledge of God: to know that we do not know Him."[27]

There is a saying frequently heard among Thomists which expresses a significant fact: Thomas feared logic as little as he feared mystery. He who fears the bold light of logic will never penetrate into the region of real mysteries. The man who does not use his reason will never get to that boundary beyond which reason really fails. In the work of St. Thomas all ways of creaturely knowing have been followed to the very end—to the boundary of mystery. And the more intensely we pursue these ways of knowledge, the more is revealed to us—of the *darkness*, but also of the *reality* of mystery.

The End Is Silence

The last word of St. Thomas is not communication but silence. And it is not death which takes the pen out of his hand. His tongue is stilled by the super-abundance of life in the mystery of God. He is silent, not because he has nothing further to say; he is silent because he has been allowed a glimpse into the inexpressible depths of that mystery which is not reached by any human thought or speech.

The acts of the canonization process record: On

the feast of St. Nicholas, in the year 1273, as Thomas turned back to his work after Holy Mass, he was strangely altered. He remained steadily silent; he did not write; he dictated nothing. He laid aside the *Summa Theologica* on which he had been working. Abruptly, in the middle of the treatise on the Sacrament of Penance, he stopped writing. Reginald, his friend, asks him, troubled: "Father, how can you want to stop such a great work?" Thomas answers only, "I can write no more." Reginald of Piperno seriously believed that his master and friend might have become mentally ill through his overwhelming burden of work. After a long while, he asks and urges once again. Thomas gives the answer: "Reginald, I can write no more. All that I have hitherto written seems to me nothing but straw." Reginald is stunned by this reply. Some time later, as he had often done before, Thomas visits his younger sister, the Countess of San Severino, near Salerno. It is the same sister who had aided Thomas in his escape from the castle of San Giovanni, nearly thirty years ago. Shortly after his arrival, his sister turns to his travelling companion, Reginald, with a startled question: what has happened to her brother? He is like one struck dumb and has scarcely spoken a word to her. Reginald once more appeals to Thomas: Would he tell him why he has ceased writing and what it is that could have disturbed him so deeply? For a long time, Thomas remains silent. Then he repeats: "All that I have written seems to me nothing but straw . . . compared to what I have seen and what has been revealed to me."

This silence lasted throughout a whole winter. The great teacher of the West had become dumb. Whatever may have imbued him with a deep happiness, with an inkling of the beginning of eternal life, must have aroused in the men in his company the disturbing feeling caused by the uncanny.

At the end of this time, spent completely in his own depths, Thomas began the journey to the General Council at Lyons. His attention continued to be directed inward. The acts of the canonization report a conversation which took place on this journey between Thomas and Reginald. It seems to have arisen out of a long silence and to have receded immediately into a long silence. This brief exchange clearly reveals to what degree the two friends already live in two different worlds. Reginald, encouragingly: "Now you are on your way to the Council, and there many good things will happen; for the whole Church, for our order, and for the Kingdom of Sicily." And Thomas: "Yes, God grant that good things may happen there!"

The prayer of St. Thomas that his life should not

outlast his teaching career was answered. On the way to Lyons he met his end.

The mind of the dying man found its voice once more, in an explanation of the Canticle of Canticles for the monks of Fossanova. The last teaching of St. Thomas concerns, therefore, that mystical book of nuptial love for God, of which the Fathers of the Church say: the meaning of its figurative speech is that God exceeds all our capabilities of possessing Him, that all our knowledge can only be the cause of new questions, and every finding only the start of a new search.

II

THE NEGATIVE ELEMENT
IN THE PHILOSOPHY
OF ST. THOMAS AQUINAS

That name which can be
pronounced is not the
Eternal Name.—LAO-TSE

Perceiving the Unexpressed

What is self-evident is not discussed. It is taken for granted; it "goes without saying." *Cela va sans dire.* One only has to ask: what exactly is it that is taken for granted and so may remain unexpressed?

In this seemingly innocent situation, which in its turn is largely taken for granted, there lies the most important and the peculiar difficulty of all textual interpretations: namely, that in a passage to be elucidated certain notions remain unexpressed because they were self-evident to the author, whereas they are in no way self-evident to the man who is interpreting the text. Consequently, he does not automatically include them in his perception. And this means that the emphasis of all he *does* perceive is changed. In the interpretation of a text, especially one from a civilization or epoch remote from our own, what is plainly decisive and yet by no means easy is this: to grasp those basic assumptions which, remaining unexpressed, nevertheless permeate all that is actually stated; to discover, so to speak, the hidden keynote that dominates whatever has been explicitly said.

It could be positively maintained that the doctrine of a thinker is precisely *"das im Sagen Ungesagte*, the unexpressed in what is expressed." This is how Heidegger begins his own interpretation of a Platonic text.[1] The phrase is no doubt deliberately strained, but it is clear that an interpretation which does not reach the unspoken assumptions underlying the actual text must remain, in essence, a misinterpretation, even if in other respects the letter of the text be commented upon with considerable learning; this latter fact may, indeed, make matters worse.

Is there a way to get on to the track of such underlying and therefore unformulated assumptions? I think there exist several such deciphering keys. One, which I have frequently verified, is certainly this. It occasionally happens that what is unexpressed shows itself, as though through a "hole," through a "gap" in the pattern, in a certain "jump" in the development of the thought, a kind of inconsequence in the argument. (This at least is how it appears to *us*, who interpret and start out with other assumptions which are just as implicit and perhaps never once explicitly formulated.) What matters is that, whenever one of these seeming illogicalities is encountered, we avoid passing over it carelessly. There will be later an opportunity to speak of one concrete instance of this kind.

The Hidden Key: Creation

In the philosophy of St. Thomas Aquinas, there is a fundamental idea by which almost all the basic concepts of his vision of the world are determined: the idea of creation, or more precisely, the notion that nothing exists which is not *creatura*, except the Creator Himself; and in addition, that this createdness determines entirely and all-pervasively the inner structure of the creature.

As regards the "Aristotelianism" of St. Thomas Aquinas ("Aristotelianism" is a highly dubious term, to be applied with caution), we shall completely miss the significance of his turning to Aristotle, unless we consider it from the point of view of this fundamental idea, worked out to its logical consequences: namely, that all things are *creatura*, not merely soul and spirit, but also the visible world.

It may appear natural enough, scarcely worth discussion, and in any case not at all surprising, that the conceptual thinking of a theologian of the Middle Ages should be dominated by the notion of creation, even in his philosophical explanation of reality. What might cause wonder is the extent to which it is here a question of an *unexpressed* assumption, an opinion *not* explicitly formulated,

47

that has, as it were, to be read between the lines. Did not Thomas develop fully and explicitly a doctrine of creation? That naturally is true and quite well known. None the less, it is equally true, though not so well known, that the notion of creation determines and characterizes the interior structure of *nearly all* the basic concepts in St. Thomas's philosophy of Being. And this fact is *not* evident; it is scarcely ever put forward explicitly; it belongs to the unexpressed in St. Thomas's doctrine of Being. This element has remained so unnoticed that the textbook interpretations of St. Thomas hardly once mention it. Indeed, this customary interpretation of St. Thomas has been considerably determined by Rationalist thought,[2] which is shown not least by the silence on this particular point that has inevitably led to misunderstandings with grave consequences. For instance, the meaning of propositions such as "all that exists is good," or "all that exists is true," is misunderstood, as is, in my opinion, the general significance of the so-called "transcendental" concepts (in the traditional sense)—unless it be realized that the concepts and theses in question do not refer to a neutral Being that simply exists, not to an *ens ut sic*, not to an indeterminate world of "objects," but formally to Being as *creatura*. That things are good precisely because they exist, and that this goodness is identical with the Being of

things and is no mere property attached to them;
that further, the term "true" is a synonym for
"existing,"[3] and therefore that what exists is true
by virtue of its existence, and does not first of all
exist and then, in a secondary sense, become also
true—these ideas, which belong no doubt to the
basis of the classical ontological doctrine of the
West and have been formulated with rare genius
by St. Thomas, *must*—if we fail to consider reality
and objects formally as created—simply lose their
full savor. They become shallow, sterile and tautol-
ogous—as has actually been for this very reason the
destiny of all these propositions, so that Kant, in a
celebrated passage in the *Critique of Pure Reason*,
was to some extent justified in eliminating them
from the philosophical vocabulary.[4]

We come now to our basic theme: St. Thomas's
doctrine of truth can be grasped in its proper and
profoundest meaning only if we bring into play
this notion of creation. And when we examine, as
we shall do here, the interrelation of the concept of
truth with the "negative element" of unknowability and mystery, we discover that this interrelation does not become manifest except through the
fundamental thought that everything which can be
made the object of human knowledge is either
creatura or Creator.

This may perhaps suggest that St. Thomas's

theory of truth is not strictly "pure philosophy" but something philosophico-theological. The question can here remain open; its answer will depend upon one's interpretation of the idea "creation." Is it philosophical or theological?

"To Be True" Means to Be Creatively Thought

It is of course impossible to expound here the whole of St. Thomas's doctrine of truth in all its ramifications. It is not, however, necessary to do so in order to define the purpose of the present study. Our study will be confined in the main to the notion of the truth of things in the world, of the *veritas rerum*. This is commonly understood as "onto-logical truth" and is distinguished from "logical truth," the truth of knowledge. Yet it is not quite correct to dissociate too much these two concepts of truth. In St. Thomas's mind they are intimately linked. For example, with the common modern objection, as it has been repeatedly formulated from Bacon to Kant, "that truth can be predicated not of what really exists but, in the strict and proper sense, only of what is thought," St. Thomas would to a large extent agree. He would reply that this is quite to the point. Only what is thought can be called in the strict sense "true," but real things *are* something thought! It is essential to their nature (he would continue), that they are thought. They are real precisely *because* they are thought. To put it more explicitly, they are real because they are thought *creatively*, that is, they have been fashioned by thought. The essence of things is that they are creatively thought. This is to be taken literally and not in a figurative sense. Further, because things are themselves thoughts and have the "character of a word" (as Guardini says),[5] they may be called—in a quite precise and legitimate usage of the term—"true," in the same way as one ordinarily calls true thoughts and what is thought.

It was, as it seems, St. Thomas's view that the notion that things have an essence cannot be separated from the other notion: that this essential character is the fruit of a form-giving thought that plans, devises, and creates.

This interrelation is foreign to modern Rationalism. Why, it would argue, can we not think of the "nature" of plants and the "nature" of men without needing also to consider that these "natures" are called into being by thought? Modern thinking habits can make nothing of the suggestion that there could be no such "nature" unless it were thus creatively thought. Curiously enough, this thesis of St. Thomas has received unexpected and emphatic support in the principles of modern, indeed we might term it post-modern, Existentialism. From Sartre's radical negation of the idea of creation (he declares, for example, that "Existentialism is nothing more than an attempt to draw all the conclusions from a consistently atheistic position,")[6] it is suddenly made evident how and to what extent the doctrine of creation is the concealed but basic foundation of classical Western metaphysics. If one were to compare the thought of Sartre and St. Thomas and reduce both to syllogistic form, one would realize that both start with the same "major premise," namely from this principle: things have an essential nature only in so far as they are fashioned by thought. Since man exists and has a constructive intellect, which can invent and has in fact invented, for instance, a letter opener, therefore, and for no other reason, we can speak of the "nature" of a letter opener. Then, Sartre continues, because there exists *no* creative intelligence which could have designed man and all natural things—and could have put an inner significance into them—therefore there is *no* "nature" in things that are not manufactured and artificial. Here are his actual words: "There is no such thing as human nature because there exists no God to think it creatively."

("*Il n'y a pas de nature humaine, puisqu'il n'y a pas de Dieu pour la concevoir.*")[7] St. Thomas, on the contrary, declares: Because and in so far as God has creatively thought things, just so and to that extent have they a nature. "This very fact that a creature has its special and finite substance shows that it comes from a principle"[8]—this is a sentence from the *Summa Theologica*. What is common to Sartre and St. Thomas, it is now evident, is the assumption that we can speak of the nature of things only when they are expressly considered as *creatura.* The fact that things are creatively thought by the Creator—this is exactly what St. Thomas means when he refers to the truth that dwells in everything that is real.

THINGS CAN BE KNOWN BECAUSE THEY ARE CREATED

The basic principle in St. Thomas's doctrine of the truth of things can be found in the *Quaestiones Disputatae de Veritate.*[9] It is as follows. "*Res naturalis inter duos intellectus constituta (est)*, a natural thing is placed between two knowing subjects," namely, as he explains, between the *intellectus divinus* and the *intellectus humanus*, between the Divine and the human minds.

In this "localization" of existing things between the absolutely creative knowledge of God and the non-creative, reality-conformed knowledge of man is found the structure of all reality as a system in which the archetypes and the copies are both embraced. St. Thomas here introduces, in a *non*-quantitative sense, the old and presumably Pythagorean concept of "measure," the *mensura*, as something on the one hand given and on the other received. The creative knowledge of God gives measure but receives none (*mensurans non mensuratum*). Natural reality is at once measured and itself measuring (*mensuratum et mensurans*). But human knowledge is measured and does not give measure (*mensuratum non mensurans*); at least it is not what gives measure with respect to natural things, though it does so with regard to *res artificiales*, artificial things. (This is the point at which for St. Thomas the distinction between created and artificially constructed things comes into bearing.)

Corresponding with this double reference in things—this is the further development of St. Thomas's ideas—there must be a double concept of the "truth of things." The first denotes the creative fashioning of things by God; the second their intrinsic knowability for the human mind. The expression "things are true" means in the first place that they are creatively thought by God; in the second, that they can be approached and grasped in human knowledge. Between these two concepts of truth there exists a relation of *prioritas naturae*, an ontological precedence.

This precedence has a twofold significance. In the first place, we cannot seize the core of this notion: the "truth of things"; in fact, we miss it entirely unless we make it explicit that these things are *creatura*, that they have been brought into being by the creative knowledge of God, and that they proceed from the very "eye of God" (as the ancient Egyptian ontology expressed this same idea).

There is, however, a second meaning to this priority: it is the creative fashioning of things by God which *makes it possible* for them to be known by men. These two references are therefore connected with one another, not, as it were, like an older and younger brother, but like father and son. The former brings forth the latter. What does this signify? It signifies that things can be known by us because God has creatively thought them; *as* creatively thought by God, things have not only their *own* nature ("for themselves alone"); but *as* creatively thought by God, things have also a reality "for us." Things have their intelligibility, their inner clarity and lucidity, and the power to reveal themselves, because God has creatively thought them. This is why they are essentially intelligible. Their brightness and radiance is infused into things from the creative mind of God, together with their essential being (or rather, as the very essence of that being!). It is this radiance, and this alone, that makes existing things perceptible to human knowledge. In a scripture commentary[10] St. Thomas remarks: "The measure of the reality of a thing is the measure of its light." In a late work, the commentary on the *Liber de Causis*,[11] there is a fundamental sentence that formulates this same idea in an almost mystical phrase: "*Ipsa actualitas rei est quoddam lumen ipsius*, the reality of things is itself their light," the reality of things understood *as* created being! It is this light that makes things perceptible to our eyes. To put it succinctly, things are knowable because they have been created.

At this point something analogous to Sartre's objection against the treatment of the nature of things in eighteenth-century philosophy[12] may be said about the foundation of knowledge. Do not think that it is possible to do both, to argue away the idea that things have been creatively thought by God and then go on to understand how things can be known by the human mind!

Things Are Unfathomable Because They Are Created

In the judgment of St. Thomas, we can, therefore, in the realm of created natural reality, speak of "truth" in two different senses.

Firstly, the truth of *things* can be implied, and this means primarily that these things, as *creaturae*, correspond with the archetypal creative thought of God; it is this correspondence which formally constitutes the truth of things. Secondly, we can speak of truth with reference to *knowledge* (of man), which again is true in so far as it "receives its measure" from and corresponds to the objective reality of things. It is in this second correspondence, in turn, that the truth of human knowledge consists. These two concepts of truth are formulated in the same article of the *Summa Theologica* and are there contrasted with one another:

"When things are the norm and measure of the intellect, truth consists in the equation of the intellect to these things . . . but when the intellect is the norm and measure of things, then truth consists in the equation of things to the intellect."[13] These sentences express, from yet another point of view, the structure of all created Being—essentially situated between the creative knowledge of God and

57

man's imitative knowledge: an idea we can never fully exhaust.

Between these two relationships (that of mind to reality and, on the other hand, of reality to mind) which both, as correspondences (*adequationes*), signify in different ways "truth," there is only one fundamental distinction: one can be the object of human knowledge, the other can not; one relationship, but not the other, can be known by man.

Man is certainly in a position not only to know things, but also to understand the relationship between things and his concept of them. In other words, over and above his spontaneous perception of things, he can have knowledge by means of judgments and reflections. To put it in another way, human knowledge may not only be true, it can also be knowledge of the truth.[14]

It is very different, however, when we turn to the relationship between things and the creative mind of God, in which the truth of things primarily and properly consists, and which in its turn first renders human knowledge possible. (*Cognitio est quidam veritatis effectus;* this again is a revolutionary sentence of St. Thomas, of the kind that stands our more normal formulae on their heads: "Knowledge is a certain effect of truth," . . . indeed of the truth of things!)[15] This relation on which the truth of things is fundamentally based—the relation between natural reality and the archetypal creative thought of God—*cannot, I insist, be known formally by us.* We can of course know things; we cannot formally know their *truth.* We know the copy, but not the relation of the copy to the archetype, the correspondence between what has been designed and its first design. To repeat, we have no power of perceiving this correspondence by which the formal truth of things is constituted. Here we can notice how truth and unknowability belong together. This thought now calls for a more exact statement.

The term "unknowable" is literally capable of several or at least of *two* meanings. It can indicate something that "in itself" is capable of being known, but which a particular knowing faculty is unable to grasp because it lacks a sufficient power of penetration. In this sense, we refer to objects which "cannot be observed by the naked eye." It is a question rather of a deficiency of vision than of any special property of the object. Stars that we are unable to perceive are "in themselves" quite capable of observation. In this context, "unknowable" denotes that the particular faculty is not powerful enough to realize and make actual the possibility of being known which certainly exists. But this term "unknowable" can have another significance, namely that no such possibility of being known is given, that there is nothing to be known; that not only on the side of a particular *subject* is there a defect of apprehension and penetration, but that on the side of the *object* there is no possibility to be known.

Unknowability in the latter sense, namely that something real should in itself be unknowable, would be for St. Thomas simply preposterous. Because Being is created, that is to say creatively thought by God, it is therefore "in itself" light, radiant, and self-revealing—*precisely because it is*. Accordingly, for St. Thomas, the unknowable can never denote something in itself dark and impenetrable, but only something that has so much light that a particular finite faculty of knowledge cannot absorb it all. It is too rich to be assimilated completely; it eludes the effort to comprehend it.

It is in this latter meaning that we are now considering the term "unknowable." And I insist that it belongs immediately to the idea of the truth of things. What I want to emphasize is the following: According to the doctrine of St. Thomas, it is part of the very nature of things that their knowability cannot be wholly exhausted by any finite intellect, *because* these things are creatures, which means that the very element which makes them capable of being known must necessarily be at the same time the reason why things are unfathomable. This calls for closer analysis.

The statement "things are true" indicates primarily, as we saw, that things are creatively thought by God. This sentence, as I have previously said, would be totally misunderstood if it were taken merely as a statement about *God*, about a divine activity directed toward things. No, something is said about the structure of *things*. It is another way of expressing the view of St. Augustine,[16] that things exist because God sees them (whereas we see things because they exist). This means that the reality and character of things *consist* in their being creatively thought by the Creator. "True," as I have said before, is an ontological name, a synonym for "real." *Ens et verum convertuntur*; it is the same whether I say "something real" or whether I say "something creatively thought by God." The essence of all things (as creatures) is that they are formed after an archetypal pattern which dwells in the absolutely creative mind of God. *"Creatura in Deo est creatrix essentia,* the creature is in God creative essence." This is how St. Thomas speaks in his commentary on St. John.[17] The *Summa Theologica* contains a similar passage: "Every existing thing possesses the truth of its nature to the degree in which it imitates the knowledge of God."[18]

As we have said, St. Thomas, in his study of the truth of things, which means the *nature* of things, was obviously *unable* to ignore or "leave out" this correspondence between things and their divine exemplars. This is revealed, for example, where he reads it into texts in which our minds can discover no trace of it. The following example is an instance of that "tendency to jump," that "unevenness" in the development of an argument, in which as though through a rift in the texture, the unstated and unexpressed is revealed. In the second article of the first *Quaestio de Veritate*, St. Thomas sets forth clearly his notion of the truth of things: "What is real is called true in so far as it realizes that toward which it is ordained by the mind of God," —to phrase it differently, an existing thing is true to the extent that it reproduces the pattern of divine knowledge. This is clearly brought out (*sicut patet*), continues St. Thomas, by a famous definition of Avicenna. Yet in this definition *our* minds would detect nothing of the kind. What then does this definition of Avicenna say? It became almost classical during the Middle Ages: "The truth of every individual thing is the special character of its Being that has been given to it as its abiding possession."[19] St. Thomas reads into *this* text a confirmation of his own thesis that the truth of things consists in their being creatively thought by God. It would never have occurred to *us* to notice any connection between the two statements. This evident "gap" in his line of argument can only mean that St. Thomas was unable to separate the idea that things have an essence—a "what"—from the other idea that this essence of things is the fruit of a designing and creative knowledge.

Let me now turn back to our proper problem. We can never properly grasp this correspondence between the original pattern in God and the created copy, in which formally and primarily the truth of things consists. It is quite impossible for us, as spectators, so to speak, to contemplate the emergence of things from "the eye of God." Since this is so, our quest for knowledge, when it is directed toward the essences of things, even of the lowest and "simplest" order, must move along a pathway to which there is, in principle, no end. The reason for this is that things are *creaturae*, that the inner lucidity of Being has its ultimate and exemplary source in the boundless radiance of Divine Knowledge. This condition is included in the concept of the truth of Being as formulated by St. Thomas; its real profundity, however, is only realized when we understand it in its interrelation with the concept of creation, an interrelation which St. Thomas takes for granted.

In this concept of truth, understood as I have outlined it, the negative element of "unknowability" has its proper place and origin.

We are concerned here only with the *philosophia*

negativa of St. Thomas, although he has also laid down the principles of a *theologia negativa*. It is true that this latter fact, also, is not prominent in the traditional presentations of Thomistic doctrine; often enough it is omitted altogether. Mention is rarely made of the fact that the teaching about God in the *Summa Theologica* begins with this sentence: "We are not capable of knowing what God is, but we can know what He is *not*."[20] I know of no textbook of Thomistic thought which contains the notion expressed by St. Thomas in his commentary on the *De Trinitate* of Boethius;[21] namely, that there are three degrees in our knowledge of God: the lowest, the knowledge of God as He is active in creation; the second, the recognition of God as mirrored in spiritual beings; the third and loftiest, the recognition of God as the *Unknown*, *tamquam ignotum*. Or consider this sentence from the *Quaestiones Disputatae:* "This is what is ultimate in the human knowledge of God: to know that we do not know God," *quod (homo) sciat se Deum nescire.*[22]

As we turn to the "negative element" in St. Thomas's *philosophy*, we come across the passage about thinkers whose quest for knowledge has not succeeded in finding the essence of a single fly. This passage occurs in an almost popular exposition of the Apostles' Creed;[23] yet it stands in intimate relation with many other similar sentences.

Some of these sentences are astonishingly "negative." For example: "The essential grounds of things are unknown to us, *principia essentialia rerum sunt nobis ignota.*"[24] This formula is in no way so untypical or exceptional as it at first glance appears. It would be easy to set alongside it a dozen similar passages (from the *Summa Theologica*, the *Summa Contra Gentiles*, the *De Veritate*, and the other *Quaestiones Disputatae*):

"*Formae substantiales per se ipsas sunt ignota,*[25] we do not know substantial forms as they are in themselves. *Differentiae essentiales sunt nobis ignotae,*[26] essential differences are not known to us."

All these sentences indicate that we have no proper means of knowing the distinctive element in things, and this means the essence of things. This is the reason, St. Thomas urges, why we cannot give them a name conveying their true Being, and have to attach names to them from casual circumstances. (In this context, St. Thomas frequently makes use of the absurd etymologies current in medieval times: e.g., *lapis* (stone) from *laedere pedem,* "what hurts the foot when it stumbles against it.")[27]

Not only God Himself but also things have an "eternal name" that man is unable to utter. This is

meant precisely and not "poetically." And on this
point the traditional wisdom of the West agrees
with the quotation from the Chinese, which I intro-
duced at the beginning of this study.

What is the precise reason, asks St. Thomas in
one passage, why it is impossible for us to know
God perfectly through creation? His reply has two
parts, and it is the second that is the more interest-
ing. The first maintains that creation can represent
God only in an imperfect manner. The second adds
that our minds are too crude and obtuse (*imbecil-
litas intellectus nostri*) to read in things even that information concerning God which they really contain.[28]

To understand the force of this expression, we
must remember that in the opinion of St. Thomas
the special manner in which the Divine Perfection is imitated is what constitutes the special *essence* of a thing.

"Every creature has its own proper species (*pro-
priam speciem*) according to which it participates
in some way in the likeness of the Divine Essence.
Therefore, as God knows His Essence as so imitable
by such a creature (*ut sic imitabilem a tali creatura*),
He knows it as the particular model and idea of
that creature."[29] This thought points the way to a
new and complex problem; nevertheless it has a
close relation to our present theme. What it states is

just this: the ultimate reality of things is something to which we can never finally penetrate, because we can never fully grasp these likenesses of the Divine Ideas precisely as likenesses.

This twofold reply has a definitely dialectic structure. It reflects the structure of created reality which, by definition, has its origin from God and also from nothing. For St. Thomas not only insists that the reality of things is their light; he also says: "*Creatura est tenebra inquantum est ex nihilo*, created things are darkness in so far as they proceed from nothing." This sentence comes not from Heidegger but from the *Quaestiones Disputatae* of St. Thomas.[30] The reply to the query why we cannot know God fully from creation has the same curiously dialectic structure. What does it in fact assert? It declares the following.

Things through their essence express God only in an imperfect manner. And why? Because things are creatures and the created cannot wholly express the Creator. Nevertheless, the answer continues, the fullness of light even in this imperfect expression surpasses our power of comprehension. Again, why? Because man is himself a creature, but still more for the reason that things in their reality refer back to a divine design. And this means once again, because things are creatures.

Hope as the Structure of
Creaturely Knowledge

We have referred to the "negative element" in the philosophy of St. Thomas Aquinas. A formula of this kind can be easily misunderstood and requires a more precise statement, and perhaps even some correction.

This "negative" character is not to be understood in the sense that the Being of things cannot be attained in human knowledge. "*Intellectus . . . penetrat usque ad rei essentiam*, the mind makes its way to the essence of things,"[31]—this remains a valid proposition for St. Thomas, in spite of his assertion that the intellectual efforts of the philosophers have never been able to grasp the essence of a single fly. These two sentences belong together. That the mind *does* attain to things is proven precisely in the fact that it enters into the unfathomable light; because and to the extent that it does attain to the reality of things, it discovers that they cannot be fathomed. As Nicholas of Cusa said in his explanation of the Socratic "learned ignorance":[32] Only when a man comes into visual contact with light does he realize that the sun's brightness altogether transcends his power of vision.

With St. Thomas there can be no question of agnosticism, and Neo-Scholasticism is perfectly right in insisting upon this. But it is not possible, in my opinion, to bring out clearly the true reason for this fact, without formally bringing into play the concept of creation, i.e., the structure of things precisely as creatures. In other words, things in so far as they are creatively thought by God possess these two properties: on the one hand their ontological clarity and self-revelation and, on the other hand, their inexhaustibleness; their knowability as well as their "unknowability." Unless we go back to this basic position, we cannot, I submit, show how the "negative element" in the thought of St. Thomas is safeguarded from agnosticism. Anyone who endeavors to pass this by runs the inevitable danger of interpreting St. Thomas as a Rationalist, and therefore of misunderstanding him even more, as is illustrated by the example of some Neo-Scholastic authors who tried to reduce his teaching to a system.

It seems to me that St. Thomas's doctrine means that *hope* is the condition of man's existence as a knowing subject, a condition that by its very nature cannot be fixed: it is neither comprehension and possession nor simply non-possession, but "not-yet-possession." The knowing subject is visualized as a traveller, a *viator*, as someone "on the way." This means, from one point of view, that the steps he takes have significance, that they are not altogether in vain, and that they bring him nearer to his goal. Yet this thought has to be complemented by another: as long as man as "existing being" is "on the way," just so long is the "way" of his knowing uncompleted. This condition of hope in every philosophizing search after the nature of things, may it be said once more, is based upon the "createdness" of the world and of the knowing man himself.

Because hope is much closer to affirmation than to denial, the "negative element" in the philosophy of St. Thomas, which we set out to formulate, must be envisaged against the background of an embracing affirmation. That the essences of things are unknowable is part of the notion of the truth of Being. But so little does this denote objective inaccessibility, the impossibility of cognition, or darkness on the part of things, that there is, on the contrary, this striking paradox: In the last resort, things are inaccessible to human knowledge precisely because they are all too knowable.

There is a well-known sentence of Aristotle which says: "As the eyes of bats are dazzled by sunlight, so it is with human intelligence when face to face with what is by nature most obvious."[33] In his commentary on this sentence, Thomas thoroughly accepts its whole significance, but goes on to underline its positive aspect in this magnificent formulation: "*Solem etsi non videat oculus nycticoracis, videt tamen eum oculus aquilae,*[34] though the eyes of the bat do not avail to behold the sun, it is seen by the eye of the eagle."

III

THE TIMELINESS

OF THOMISM

At first sight the theme of this study appears self-evident and stated without ambiguity.[1] And yet this impression is somewhat deceptive. What actually is the sense of the terms "timeliness" and "Thomism?" The answer to this query is by no means simple, not to mention that we are far from any complete unanimity on the point.

The first step, then, is obvious. What do we understand by both terms?

What Is Timeliness?

Whenever it is argued that a certain doctrine is timely and of special relevance to our day and age, and whenever this quality is considered in a positive, affirmative sense, the logical premise is that man's mind is essentially conditioned by time and history. For a mind that possesses the whole of truth simultaneously, as *tota et simul possessio*, to employ the classic phrase of Boethius—for a knowing subject of time-transcending quality, for God, therefore, and perhaps for the pure intellect, there can be nothing "timely,". for the reason that everything is timely. And whenever the human mind is conceived as potentially capable of grasping at any given moment the full content of truth, and consequently man's essential nature as conditioned by time and history is denied, the notion of "timeliness" again cannot be seriously thought. Metaphysical Rationalism which prescinds from history cannot use the term "timely" in a positive sense; "timely" here becomes practically a synonym for "false" or "heretical." What is "of the moment" is suspect, has no true being, deserves no attention. It was from this premise that, during the thirteenth century, those who claimed to possess the "entire content of truth" censured Albert the Great and Thomas Aquinas as "the great moderns."

The temporal condition of the human mind, however, seems to have an additional implication, namely, that man, in his history, whether it be individual or collective, does not advance through a continuous process of development like a plant, from a state of inferior to one of greater and more comprehensive understanding. Rather, the actual historical development of the human intellect appears as a progress in the form of assertion and counter-assertion. The assertion does not seize upon the totality of truth in one gradual, uninterrupted process, but, expressing one aspect of truth, necessarily conceals another. The second aspect is brought out in the counter-assertion, which interrupts the assertion until in its turn it is interrupted. As one aspect of the varied and many-sided truth becomes more evident, another aspect in turn recedes from view. And when this other aspect forces its way back from oblivion into consciousness, the earlier aspect tends to fade from the mind. The law underlying this process is concealed from us; it cannot be known in advance or once and for all. The fact that every positive chance involves at the same time a danger shows in the clearest possible manner that the human mind can enjoy no *tota et simul possessio*. Indeed no positive chance can be taken without accepting the risk inherent in it. Consequently it becomes evident that the human mind is essentially finite, time-conditioned, and historical.

But are we not engaged in discussing the concept of timeliness? Actually, we are trying to bring into focus the ambiguity of this concept. If the historical character of knowledge implies that in a particular epoch certain elements of the truth emerge into prominence more definitely than in other times, that therefore certain problems and tasks have greater urgency, that for the same reason other elements of the truth recede and are in danger of being forgotten—how are we to determine what is "relevant" and "timely" in this particular age?

To begin with, everything is obviously timely and relevant which encourages and confirms an epoch in its special values, attitudes and problems, which positively and immediately corresponds with the line of its major effort. But here we should not forget that such an emphasis on the primarily discussed concerns of an epoch must intensify the blind spots of that epoch. This suggests a further notion of "timeliness": timely is not only what an epoch "wants," but also what an epoch "needs"; a corrective attitude to the present is timely, the refusal to accept it is timely, or, rather, the refusal of the dangers necessarily inherent in its chances.

Consequently, both the "timely" and the "untimely," in the immediate sense of these terms, may be relevant to an epoch. When Nietzsche gave his challenging essay, *Of the Use and Disadvantage of History for Life*, the title, "Untimely Meditations," he knew, and rightly, that they were of the greatest relevance to his time. In the fact that the "untimely" may be experienced as supremely "timely," that man's limited condition can be grasped as limitation, we find, however, another proof of something new and different: that the human mind, in spite of its strict historical boundaries, is not the prisoner of a specific period; rather, that it is truly spirit, *capax universi*, oriented toward the whole of truth, and therefore capable of detached consideration even of its own time-conditioned existence.

From the start, then, the notion of timeliness contains a note of optimism, of confidence. It is the confidence that each "contemporary" emphasis upon some special feature of truth need not imply a denial of the totality of truth (as every shade of Rationalism tends arrogantly to assume); that, on the contrary, this emphasis might bring with it the chance for a new perception of truth. This chance, as we have seen, is by its nature linked with its inherent danger. We may therefore reach the conclusion that the notion of timeliness includes an element of vigilant confidence in what happens at the moment to be "modern."

From what has gone before it becomes evident how presumptuous is the undertaking to propose an answer to the question: "What is relevant and timely in our present day and age?" Even supposing that the present age provided a uniform pattern, who would be in a position to say what the age "wants" and what it "needs"; in other words, who could say what is timely and relevant and also what is relevant though untimely? In view of what is happening today in the world, who could achieve the right blend of critical detachment and immediate identity with his time?

For this reason, I am anxious, from the start, to state the limitations of what follows. My intention is merely to consider the problem from this particular angle.

WHAT IS THOMISM?

The term "Thomism" has many meanings. Let us begin by saying what we do *not* understand by it.

I am, first of all, not concerned with that very special Thomism which, in the teaching on supernatural grace, is contrasted with "Molinism." Nor am I dealing with Thomism as it is generally distinguished from "Suarezianism." These are, strictly speaking, various modes of interpretation of St. Thomas. A celebrated discussion between Martin Grabmann and Franz Pelster at the International Thomistic Congress in Rome in 1925 made it evident that the most important of the controverted doctrines, that of the real distinction between essence and existence, had for St. Thomas himself only a subordinate value, and that his earliest pupils thought it possible and legitimate to interpret it in *several* ways. Whatever the correct solution of this complicated question may be, both interpretations, the "Suarezian" as well as the one which calls itself "Thomistic," recognize explicitly the authority of

St. Thomas. Undoubtedly the divergence between them is less significant than their agreement.

How then are we to understand Thomism in this discussion of its timeliness? We will take the term in its broad current usage as the designation of all forms of Thomistic discipleship, and particularly of the world view elaborated in the works of St. Thomas. Thomism in this sense means nothing more nor less than the teaching of St. Thomas.

But here let me observe immediately that this is a questionable and problematic term, justified though we may be in using it, in view of the shortcomings of the human vocabulary.

However vaguely the term Thomism may be applied in general usage, it contains undoubtedly some elements of interpretation which may easily lead to an erroneous idea of the teaching of St. Thomas. Leo Tolstoi has said that the philosophy of a "Tolstoyan" would inevitably be completely foreign to his own philosophy. I would not venture to suggest that St. Thomas might have made a similar statement about a Thomist. Yet one can readily see how suspect the designation "Thomism" becomes. Why is it so inappropriate? Because it leads us to think almost automatically of a specific school of thought elaborated in polemical theses and counter-theses, and particularly of a traditionally perpetuated teaching system of propositions.

But it would seem to me quite impossible to compress the doctrine of St. Thomas into the framework of a "school" system of propositions, *unless one leaves out something of fundamental importance*. The majestic elaboration of thought manifested in St. Thomas's work is far too rich for such treatment and also far too flexible. The richness consists not alone in the fact that the theological wisdom of the earliest Christian centuries is interwoven with the philosophical heritage of the Greek world; and this is not confined to Aristotle only—there are threads from Plato also, and even from the Neo-Platonists (an author almost as often quoted by St. Thomas as Aristotle is that mysterious Syrian disciple of Plotinus who had great prestige in the West under the name of Dionysius the Areopagite). It is, I say, not this abundance of content alone which constitutes the richness of St. Thomas's work—it rests also on the fact that this process of assimilation develops on the ground of a spirituality which is altogether patterned on the teachings of Scripture and the sacramental and liturgical life of the Church. The end result is a structure of the highest intellectual order, but not in any way a closed system of school propositions.

Accordingly, St. Thomas has this in common with other truly great teachers, that he cannot easily be appropriated as the head of a specific school of thought, as the patron of an "ism." The "isms" are wont to be exclusive, and in controversy they are as "precise" and "distinct" as possible. The truly great masters, on the other hand, because of their deeper appreciation of what is unfathomable in truth, much prefer to emphasize what is common to differing positions than what is peculiar to each. They have no love for controversy. Their preference is for the more flexible and natural idiom and not for a fixed and artificial terminology. For example, all the "isms" that attach themselves to St. Thomas regard "Augustinianism" as the common adversary. But what is the attitude of St. Thomas himself? It is true that he nowhere speaks of an identity of outlook with St. Augustine. However, when he deals with the problem of divine illumination in human knowledge—one of the matters most hotly debated between Thomists and Augustinians—he states that the divergence between Augustine and himself is of no great significance, *non multum refert.*[2] It is very unlikely that an author so little interested in his own "individuality" could be readily compressed within a scholastic system without losing what is essential to his thought. Who, for instance, would venture to formulate in abstract propositions all that Plato states in the *Symposium* about the nature of love? The comparison with Plato is not as far-fetched as it might appear. In my opinion, it belongs to the essence of St. Thomas's teaching that the scholastic *articulus* has retained, and not merely in external form, the character of a genuine conversation or dialogue, that is, the character of reflective meditation, which makes no claim to possessing a definitively formulated answer. An analysis of that remarkable and almost inexhaustible first article of the *Quaestiones Disputatae de Veritate* demonstrates that no pat, unequivocal, textbook reply is given to the query: "What is truth?" Rather, St. Thomas first develops his own ingenious interpretation, and then, with rare modesty, works it into the garland of traditional definitions of truth in a web of reciprocal illumination and confirmation. Not one of the traditional formulae is rejected entirely or accepted as exclusively valid. Though they are in no way fully concordant, he can appreciate the partial validity of each. What actually is happening here? It happens that St. Thomas is, in effect, placing himself within the stream of traditional truth nourished by the past; without claiming to give a final solution, he leaves the way open for future quest and discovery as that stream flows onward toward the yet unknown. This is exactly the method of the Platonic dialogues. A similar conclusion is reached in recent studies on the theory of knowledge in St. Thomas. They prove that

Thomas quite evidently deliberately refrained from giving a dogmatic definition of knowledge.

All this should make sufficiently clear why it seems to me highly questionable to treat the teaching of St. Thomas as an "ism," and why we should use the term "Thomism" only with important reservations.

It might well be said that by this very structure the teaching of St. Thomas is relevant to our time, in the sense both of timeliness and untimeliness. It might be said that the timeliness of St. Thomas rests to a large extent on the fact that there can be no such thing as "Thomism." This remark, I realize, requires elaboration. But before attempting this, we have to consider briefly the actual situation of modern philosophical thought.

FROM KIERKEGAARD TO SARTRE: DISTRUST OF SYSTEMATIC PHILOSOPHY

The term that immediately challenges us here is "Existentialism," though there are some other dominant trends in contemporary thought (as, for example, symbolic logic). Existentialism, as everybody knows, has become so much a fashionable term that its substance appears all but eroded; it may mean practically anything to everybody, with the result that it means nothing precise and definite to anyone. Yet we have to admit that under the name of Existentialism, the most vital and genuine philosophical thinking is being carried on today. Further, that it has a common and valid core in all its forms. This common core consists, above all, in the rejection and distrust of the rationalistic systems of philosophy. This unites Sartre, Marcel, Heidegger with the ancestor they have in common, Sören Kierkegaard, whose opposition against Hegel was based, precisely, on the following premise: It is not within man's scope to achieve, within a closed system of propositions, a fully sufficient reflection of the essential reality of the world; philosophy cannot, as Hegel claimed for it, change its proper title, which signifies "the loving quest for wisdom," to "actual knowledge"; it is beyond human capacity to fathom the inconsistency of the world, to uncover the hidden consistency and to formulate it in a rationally constructed "synthesis."

If, since the advent of Kierkegaard, the poetic essay and the philosophical journal have become the preferred media of expression for all forms of Existentialism, the reason for this is the conviction that an abstract, generalized thesis cannot reach to the depth of reality and that, contrary to its claim, no philosophical proposition can adequately express the "true being" of things.

In modern Existentialism this basic conviction has passed over from the narrow circle of professional thinkers into the general mentality of our present age. It finds expression in widely different attitudes, ranging from a believing reverence before the unknowable to complete agnosticism, and finally, to nihilism. It is important to notice that even in its extreme formulation, in the atheistic nihilism of Sartre ("There is no such thing as human nature— *il n'y a pas de nature humaine*")[3] this element can be found. Sartre insists that one cannot speak of the nature of man in the same authoritative manner in which one speaks of the nature of some technical instrument, the design of which is known to us, whereas we do not know the design of man.

THOMAS AQUINAS: NEGATIVE PHILOSOPHY

I am not of the opinion that the timeliness of St. Thomas's doctrine rests on the fact that it too is "existentialist." It can, however, be demonstrated that this common concern of all the Existentialisms finds in St. Thomas's teaching both a positive correspondence and a specific corrective.

Let me speak first of the positive correspondence. Medieval scholastics in general and St. Thomas in particular tend to be represented as though they were the first thinkers to achieve the ideal of a closed philosophical system. The *Summa* is taken as an example of the claim of human intelligence not only to construct an enclosed system of knowledge, but what is much more, to bring even the truths of revelation into a lucid and closely interrelated structure by means of rational proofs. The historical growth of this false and misleading picture is not easy to follow. No doubt many factors cooperated to produce it, and these factors have acted and reacted on one another. Opponents as well as followers have contributed to the misconception: not only the mistrust of natural reason characteristic of Augustinianism during the Reformation period, but also the efforts of Neo-Scholasticism to preserve its master, Thomas, from every taint or charge of agnosticism are responsible.

Curiously enough, it is rarely noticed that the *Summa Theologica* is unfinished. The normal explanation offered is that its author died so early a death. "Snatched away by death he had to leave his work incomplete," this or similar notes appear in the editions of the *Summa*. In actual fact, St. Thomas refused to conclude the work because of his own inner experiences. "I can write nothing more: all that I have hitherto written seems to me nothing but straw." This surely indicates that its fragmentary character belongs to the total implication of the *Summa Theologica*. If one does not consider this point and regards Thomas as some kind of forerunner of the systematic thinkers of modern Rationalism (Christian Wolff, the philosopher of the German *Aufklärung*, in fact claimed Thomas as his predecessor and felt in closer communion with him than with his own immediate teacher, Leibniz), it will come as a highly surprising experience to find in St. Thomas a sentence such as the following: "*Principia essentialia rerum sunt nobis ignota*, the essential principles of things are unknown to us."[4]

Such a proposition is not only far removed from the neat, well-rounded perfection of a rationalistic system, it also paraphrases a notion of philosophy that formally *excludes* the idea of a closed system. Since the distinguishing mark of a philosophical question is that it is an inquiry *into* those very *principia essentialia*, into the "essences" of things together with their deepest roots and their ultimate significance, this sentence of St. Thomas (not the only instance of its kind) makes us understand that a philosophical question cannot be answered in fully sufficient form. It cannot be answered in the same sense in which it was asked. We now realize why St. Thomas in his commentary had nothing to oppose to the passage from Aristotle's *Metaphysics* which declares that the problem of Ousia or Reality, the problem of the essences of things, is one that "in the past, today and always, was, is, and will continue to be asked and debated,"[5] which means that here is a problem that will never be finally and irrevocably solved. And one understands that Thomas can say with Aristotle: The knowledge which is pursued in the philosophical doctrine of Being, that is, the knowledge about the essence of things, is not given to man as his possession but only as a kind of "loan," *non ut possessio sed sicut aliquid mutuatum.*[6]

How, we ask ourselves, can such knowledge, which is held as a "loan," be expressed concretely? In the form of conjecture and allusion? Metaphorically or essayistically? Least of all, doubtless, in the form of a scholastic system which by its very nature has the character of a permanent possession rather than that of a loan.

It seems hardly necessary to point out here once again to what extent a fundamental postulate of contemporary philosophical thought finds its correspondence and confirmation in the work of the "Universal Doctor" of Christendom; to what ex-

tent this *philosophia negativa* of St. Thomas is
timely, timely in the sense of being a positive cor-
relate. To make this evident is not a question of
exalting St. Thomas. We are not engaged in his de-
fense. This is no matter of apologetics. What matters is the initiation of a fruitful dialogue between
the "*Zeitgeist*" and the traditional wisdom of the
Occident—a dialogue in which sterile controversies
apt to flare up among the late followers of "isms"
might be dissolved and out'of which might grow
the readiness to accept the negative counterform
of timeliness, St. Thomas's corrective "No" addressed to our time.

A Note on Created Things
and Artifacts

The various forms of "Existentialism" are, in their
turn, a necessary and salutary repudiation of their
own era. And in this, they are reinforced by St.
Thomas.

The world in which man today leads his ordi-
nary life is becoming more and more a purely technological one. The things with which he is concerned are artificial; they are artifacts, not creations.

The danger inherent in this situation is that man might, erroneously, come to regard the world as a whole and the created things with it—above all, man himself—in the same manner in which he regards, correctly, his own artifacts belonging to the technological sphere; in other words, man is beginning to consider the whole of creation as completely fathomable, fully accessible to rational comprehension, and, above all, as something which it is permissible to change, transform, or even destroy.

Engels, in a misconclusion which is well-nigh classical, infers from the productibility of artificial things the possibility of exhaustive knowledge of all natural reality ("practical experience, i.e., experimental research and industry" have brought about "the most crushing refutation" of the philosophical "fallacy" which denies "the possibility of an exhaustive knowledge" of the world)[7]—a misconclusion which for good reasons has been formally accepted into the official doctrine of Bolshevism.[8]

In opposition, contemporary Existentialism, for instance Sartre, stresses forcefully the difference between artificial and natural things. A new emphasis appears here which seems to me post-modern, while the properly "modern" thinking hardly perceives and certainly does not stress this difference.

Properly modern thinking inclines to what it believes to be a specifically "realistic" view—a view which does not emphasize the difference between immediate reality and man-made things, but tends to see forest, river, fields *and* housing development, bridge, factory as one and the same reality, as "the world around us," *our* world.

St. Thomas, on the contrary, likewise distinguishes clearly and unequivocally between the *res naturalis* and the *res artificialis*, for a reason not unlike that of the Existentialists. The *res artificialis* received its "measure" from man, but not so the *res naturalis*. St. Thomas would agree with Sartre in his warning of contemporary man against the dangers of a purely technological environment: Do not think that you can speak in the same manner about the "nature" of man as you may about the "nature" of a letter opener, the design of which has come out of your own head. Sartre, however, spoils the force and validity of this warning when he adds that there is no such thing as a "design" for man, and therefore, no "human nature." The inescapable conclusion is that you can make what you like of yourself and of man.[9]

It is at this point that the negative relevance of St. Thomas's teaching, its "untimely timeliness," appears.

What is the reason why St. Thomas states that the true Being of natural things is unfathomable, that the philosophical question cannot, in the last resort, be answered? Why does he say that it is impossible to express the essential reality of the world fully and exhaustively? In the first instance, this reason can still be framed in complete accord with Existentialism: We cannot wholly grasp the design, the archetypal pattern, of natural things.

From this formulation arise a number of considerations. In the first place, both St. Thomas and Sartre bring "design" and "essence" into the closest contact: where there is no design, there can be no essence. Things have an essence only in so far as they have been fashioned by a form-creating, knowing mind. In this sentence, too, there is a meeting of pre-modern and post-modern thought. In criticizing the philosophical atheism of the eighteenth century Sartre shows that he is in full agreement with the old doctrine of Being. It betrays, he declares, a sad lack of clear and logical thinking, when the concept of creation is abandoned but not the habit of talking about the "nature of things," as though on that point nothing had changed. It is superficial, unreasonable, and even absurd to maintain that there is a "nature" of things, anterior to existence, unless one holds at the same time that things are *creatures*.[10]

We touch now upon a second point. The verdict of St. Thomas that the design and essence of natural things cannot be wholly grasped by the human mind does not imply that these things are in no sense knowable. The essence of things, insists St. Thomas, cannot be completely grasped but it is not unknowable. Man's intellectual power enables him to penetrate to the essence of things; there can be, therefore, insights and assertions concerning the nature of things which, though not exhaustive, are nevertheless true. A true answer can be given to the question: what is the deepest significance of Being.

It is at this point that the fundamental thesis of Existentialism is repudiated. It is not, however, in refutation, in the mere fact of negation, that the timeliness of St. Thomas's teaching, as a corrective, consists. So much is clear: negation by itself is not sufficient. A corrective implies that there exists a genuine and specific correlation with the confronted thought. In what, then, consists this (negative) relevance? Precisely in this, that for St. Thomas, one and the same factor explains both why things cannot be entirely grasped and why they can be known. St. Thomas shows that the inscrutability of things is almost the same as their knowability.

This common root, to express it as briefly as possible, is the *createdness* of things, i.e., the truth that the designs, the archetypal patterns of things, dwell within the Divine Logos. Because things come forth from the eye of God, they partake wholly of the nature of the Logos, that is, they are lucid and limpid to their very depths. It is their origin in the Logos which makes them knowable to men. But because of this very origin in the Logos, they mirror an *infinite* light and can therefore not be wholly comprehended. It is not darkness or chaos which makes them unfathomable. If a man, therefore, in his philosophical inquiry, gropes after the essence of things, he finds himself, by the very act of approaching his object, in an unfathomable abyss, but it is an abyss of *light*. Asking the question of the essence of things, he also asks the question of their design and archetype, and with this he sets out on a principially endless way. If I restrict myself to inquiry into the chemical composition of a sheet of paper or the structure of an atom, I remain within the confines of an essentially answerable problem, in the sphere of definitive solutions. It is the sphere to which the sciences properly restrict themselves. But as soon as I glance, for example, at my pen, and begin to ask: What is this object?—not in the sense of expecting an answer such as: this is a tool, or, this is gold, but rather: "What is this portion of material reality in its truth and essence?"—as soon as I ask this in the true philosophical sense, I immediately and formally deal with the unfathomable and inscrutable; and this *because* it is in the nature of my question to approach to the roots of things, that is, to advance to the source of Being, the dimension of invention and form-giving design, in other words: the dimension of createdness.

What then is the reason why the philosophical question can receive no adequate answer? Why are real things, all real things, incapable of being finally grasped? (For to grasp, to comprehend a thing means to know it as completely as it is in itself knowable; to transform what is knowable in things, with no omission whatsoever, into actual knowledge, so that nothing remains which is not positively *in actu*. It is for a comprehensive answer of this sort that the philosophical question is naturally seeking.) Why is a finite spirit unable to acquire, in the last resort, such a comprehensive knowledge? The answer is: *because the knowability of Being, which we are attempting to transform into knowledge, consists in its being creatively thought by the Creator.*

Hence our human knowledge is not confronted

by a barrier of darkness; rather, there exists no sharply drawn frontier to which our mind can attain, and for this reason no "closed system" of philosophy is possible. But by this repudiation of closed systematic formulation, I am not suggesting that the wholeness of philosophy is to be lost in a chaos of confused questioning. The very light which, because it cannot be exhausted, invalidates the exclusive claims of any closed philosophical system, itself makes possible a highly coherent structure of thought. The fact that it derives from an ultimately inexhaustible divine Source, spurs us on in the performance of the philosophical act to a hope that strives toward the infinite.

In what then consists, positively and negatively, the timeliness of St. Thomas's teaching? The answer: Inasmuch as we make our own the fundamental truths which it contains, we are enabled to recognize more deeply the "chance" of truth in contemporary philosophy and to accept it. Inasmuch as this "chance" is more deeply grasped and reasonably established, we are enabled—and this is more important—to show that the inherent dangers of contemporary philosophy are capable of being overcome, instead of having to be rejected as simply negative.

This one indication cannot of course exhaust the timeliness of St. Thomas's teaching. We might ex-

amine many another thesis which, both from the
positive and the negative viewpoint, would be as
timely as his teaching that the philosophical quest
for truth is conditioned by hope. The notion of
bonum commune, for instance, as St. Thomas understands it, appears to me of immediate political
relevance in a world which is becoming increasingly
a "totalitarian world of labor." The same is true,
and for similar reasons, of the doctrine of *Natural
Law*. Or, since the attention of modern philosophy
is being particularly attracted by *philosophical an-
thropology*, it would repay attention to note the
fact that the most voluminous section of the *Summa
Theologica*, the second part, is constructed as a
study of man and of man's "true image." But all
this can be touched upon here only in passing.

THE END OF "PURE" PHILOSOPHY

Let us again consider the opinion of St. Thomas
concerning the inner structure of philosophy. It has
been made evident that a dialogue between Thomas
and contemporary Existentialists is possible only
when the theological foundations of philosophical
thinking are brought into play. Here, I believe, is

yet another reason for the timeliness of St. Thomas: He accepts no such thing as a "pure" philosophy—a notion that is equally rejected by contemporary thought. Thomas has, of course, clearly distinguished between knowledge and faith, between philosophy and theology. To have established and maintained this distinction is considered his foremost achievement. Nevertheless, there is no "philosophy of St. Thomas" that can be presented in complete detachment from his theology.

The philosophical question aims at the mystery of the world; it is concerned with what things fundamentally are. What then does the term "fundamentally" mean? Thomas's answer (this we have tried to develop) is that "fundamentally" means "in the Logos." When Platonists are speaking of the "Ideal Forms," then Thomas is speaking, as he himself declares, in the same sense, of the Divine Logos. Thomas's exact words bring this out more explicitly:[11] "In place of these Ideal Forms (*loco harum idearum*) we have one only: the Son and Word of God."[12] In their respective interpretations of the world, the same "place" that is occupied in Platonism by the doctrine of the archetypes of all things and the soul, is taken in Western Christian ontology by the doctrine of the Logos, by the doctrine of the creative "art" of God "enriched with all primeval living forms," to quote the splendid formula of

Augustine.[13] How, under conditions such as these, could philosophical reflection be kept "pure" and unaffected by theology?

On the other hand, what is characteristic and stimulating and truly "timely" in Existentialist thought from Kierkegaard to Heidegger, Marcel and Sartre, is precisely this, that the ultimate positions are explicitly brought into view; although there is often enough no question of "theology" in the proper sense. Nevertheless, when Sartre, for example, maintains that there are no "essences" of natural things, and above all no "essence" of man, *because* there exists no creative God who could have designed them,[14] it is evident that he is establishing this fundamental thesis of his philosophy on an "article of belief." And it is clear that true philosophy can come into being only when it refers to a true theology. However, we can observe from the formal structure of contemporary Existentialism that a "pure" philosophy carefully separated from theology fails to satisfy men at the present time. When we consider the origin and archetypes of Western philosophical speculation, as conceived by Plato, who found the perfection of philosophy in a turning to myth and the ancients; as conceived by Aristotle, who named the philosophical doctrine of Being "theology"; as conceived by Augustine, for whom the true philosophical act begins with an act of faith—when we consider these seminal forms of the Western quest for knowledge, we realize that they might achieve a timeliness at once affirmative and corrective in the doctrine of St. Thomas Aquinas; the reason being that this teaching is their most sober, most sharply defined, most decisively unifying realization. If only the structure of this doctrine were presented more clearly and convincingly before the minds of contemporary man!

"Thomism" as an Attitude

In considering the teaching of St. Thomas, we should not understand it merely as the material substance of an explicitly formulated set of doctrines. Much too rarely does one remember that the substance of content has its origin in a very special attitude of St. Thomas, human as well as intellectual, not only in the sense that this attitude colors the work with its particular emphasis, but also in the sense that without this special human attitude, what has been written might never have been written at all.

Should we therefore not consider this attitude, this temper of mind—though Thomas himself never expressly formulated it—as part and parcel of the spirit of the *ratio*[15] of the Universal Doctor of Christendom—the bold intrepidity which impelled and enabled the young mendicant friar at the University of Paris to "re-cognize" the truth of the Aristotelian world view, to re-integrate it as an essential part into the intellectual heritage of the Christian West, undaunted by the opposition of the defenders of traditional doctrine. And should we not see in the personal "style" of this bold recognition of truth and reality likewise an element of "timeliness," in the sense of an exemplary attitude?

A Thomism which limits itself to the consideration of the material substance of the explicitly said necessarily proves itself inadequate in a time which confronts man with wholly new problems and brings him into contact with realities previously barely glimpsed. In times such as these it is imperative to call to mind the qualities which made Thomas what he was: the all-inclusive, fearless strength of his affirmation, his generous acceptance of the whole of reality, the trustful magnanimity of his thought. And we find occasion, also, to remember: The formal and theoretical justification for this attitude is found precisely in Thomas's doctrine of the infinitely many-sided truth of things. Truth cannot be exhausted by any (human) knowledge; it remains therefore always open to new formulation.

On the other hand, what we call here the "Thomist attitude" would have to include, in order to remain true to its master, the resolution not to relinquish a single particle of the heritage of truth; for it is the hallmark of the "modernity" of Albert and Thomas that both refused to disrupt and abandon, for the sake of new ideas, the realm of tradition; they relinquished neither the Bible nor Augustine (nor, consequently, Plato) for the sake of Aristotle.

The new territory which awaits conquest today —or, more exactly, which is conquered already but not yet appropriated and put to use by philosophical speculation—is of virtually immeasurable scope. Some of its provinces may be singled out, however. Firstly, there are the new realms opened up by physics and biology. Secondly, the new dimension of the psyche brought into view by the findings of depth psychology. Thirdly, the wisdom of the East, ready for and apparently in want of absorption into the intellectual structure of Christian philosophical interpretation and the Christian way of life—or it may also be that it is we who need enrichment through this wisdom, in a quite particular manner.

In this whole context, Thomas Aquinas might attain to a new timeliness, both affirmative and corrective.

It is not as an individual "great thinker," not as "a man of genius," that Thomas is apportioned that remarkable authority the extent and claim of which is often surprising. Thomas Aquinas has something of the status of an "institution." We find him cited, in one of the great classical legal compendia, the *Codex Juris Canonici,* as a standard of orthodoxy. An encyclical of a recent Pope states that the Church accepts his teaching as her own. The same encyclical, however, warns us explicitly against the dangers of sterile imitation and shows no intention to perpetuate what was time-conditioned in Thomas's work. But it expresses beyond doubt that in his teaching—as distinct from the work of other saintly Christian teachers—the body of human traditional wisdom, in short, truth, has found expression in an entirely venerable and eminently exemplary manner.

In what, precisely, this exemplary manner consists, is not as easily demonstrable. For those who see in the unique position of St. Thomas more than the accidental effect of the forces of tradition, more than a disciplinary act of ecclesiastical politics aimed at "intellectual uniformity"—may find themselves faced again and again with the question: what precisely caused St. Thomas to become the *Doctor Communis?*

We may leave aside, as irrelevant, the skeptical question in how far an author of the long-vanished thirteenth century can be of timely interest. But another thought arises, with heightened emphasis: the decisive element in truth is not its timeliness but its truth. What then is the use of this endeavor to secure the sanction of timeliness for truth, as if truth were in need of such sanction?

The answer to this question has several facets. It is evident that timeliness, in itself, is no criterion for truth. But it is equally evident that the trueness of truth and the timeliness of truth are strikingly correlated.

To begin with, only truth can be truly timely. Only truth can correspond to chances and dangers of any given epoch—correspond as both affirmation and corrective.

On the other hand, the fullness of truth can never be grasped by a neutral and indifferent mind, but only by a mind seeking the answer to a serious and urgent existential problem. But this urgency can only be roused by an immediately experienced, real situation, of the individual and the community. This means that the truth will be more profoundly known *as* truth, the more vigorously its *timeliness* comes to light; it also means that a man experiencing his own time with a richer intensity of heart and fuller spiritual awareness has a better chance of experiencing the illuminating force of truth. Together with its timeliness, by which the responsive power of truth is focused on the immediate present, the eternal validity of truth which, incomparably compelling, transcends the whole of time, would become manifest.[10]

This makes clear the twofold, never-ending task of the true teacher: to reflect the totality of truth *and*, in a constantly inquiring meditation, to discover and point out wherein lies the relevance of truth to his own time.

POSTSCRIPT

The second and third essay of the present book provide a contribution to a discussion; one might almost say, to a debate. This has to be borne in mind, if their point is not to be missed.

A discussion implies, among other things, that what the speakers are agreed upon recedes into the background. Complete agreement rules out discussion. But "polyphony" presupposes that each partner maintains throughout his own point of view.

What has been expressed here is what one individual has thought worth contributing. This does not imply that he disagrees on all points with his interlocutors or even with his opponents. Yet he considers it valuable and even necessary to add his particular voice to the common choir.

To be more explicit: "Human knowledge is at the same time true and not fully sufficient (inadequate)." The acceptance of this sentence, for instance, provides a common ground for the author of these "essays" and a large number of his opponents in debate. This sentence, as is well known, is commonly quoted in philosophical manuals and textbooks in the proper context. But the climate of opinion in such publications is conditioned primarily by the first, positive clause of the rather contradictory thesis. This is understandable and to a certain degree inevitable. Textbooks are concerned with transmitting teachings and "solutions"; that is their character and function. But indispensable though these textbooks of philosophy are, they present at the same time, and quite naturally so, the danger, not of denying, but of veiling the inadequacy of our knowledge.

For this reason, the emphasis in the present essays has been placed on the "negative" clause of the sentence in question.

The inadequacy of human knowledge acquires an increasing significance the more we leave the field of scientific inquiry and enter the field of philosophy. This should not be interpreted to mean that in the realm of philosophy no "positive" results and answers capable of being organized into a body of teaching can be reached; they can be reached. However: the answers to a properly philosophical, which means metaphysical inquiry cannot have the same finality as a scientific solution. The inquiry into the fundamental nature of knowledge, for instance, cannot be answered in the same conclusive manner as the question: which is the germ of a specific disease? Further, the answers that can be reached in the process of philosophical inquiry are not sufficient to build up a complete "system." As Thomas has said in his *Commentary on the Metaphysics of Aristotle*, only a modest portion, a *modicum* of results, can be gathered in the philosophical inquiry concerned with the doctrine of Being—though this modest portion is of far greater weight than whatever else may be discovered by the sciences.[1]

It is with this in mind that, in the present book, emphasis has been placed not so much on the positive attainments of philosophical thought but rather on a no less important result: namely, that man, in his philosophical inquiry, is faced again and again with the experience that reality is unfathomable, and Being is mystery—an experience, it is true, which urges him not so much to communication as to silence. But it would not be the silence of resignation and still less of despair. It would be the silence of reverence.

CHRONOLOGICAL TABLE

1193 (?) Birth of St. Albertus Magnus

1194 Birth of the Emperor, Frederick II

1221 Death of St. Dominic

1224 Founding of the University of Naples by Frederick II

1224 (1225?) Birth of St. Thomas Aquinas at the castle of Roccasicca near Naples

1226 Death of St. Francis of Assisi

1226 Coronation of St. Louis (IX), King of France

1230–39 Thomas at Monte Cassino

1239 Thomas arrives at the University of Naples

1244 Thomas enters the Dominican Order

1244–45 His imprisonment in Castel San Giovanni

1245 Council of Lyons. Deposition of Frederick II

1245 Thomas comes to Paris. Beginning of the teaching activity of St. Albertus Magnus

1248 Thomas goes with Albert to Cologne. Laying of the cornerstone for Cologne Cathedral

1250 Death of Frederick II

ca. 1250 Completion of the cathedral of Notre Dame at Paris (west façade)

1252 Thomas returns to Paris as Baccalaureus. *On Es-*

sence and Existence (1254–56). *Commentary on the Sentences of Peter Lombard* (1254–56).

1254–73 Interregnum in Germany

1256 Thomas receives from the chancellor of Notre Dame permission to begin an independent and open teaching course as full professor on the same day as St. Bonaventure. *De Veritate* (1256–59). *Commentary on Isaias* (1256–59). *Commentary on Boethius's De Trinitate* (1257–58)

1259 Thomas goes to Italy. *Summa Contra Gentiles* (1259–64)

1260–64 Thomas serves as teacher in the college of the papal court under Urban IV. *Office for the feast of Corpus Christi* (1264)

1264 Death of Urban IV. Thomas goes to Rome. *De Potentia Dei* (1265–67). *Summa Theologica* (1266–73)

1265 Birth of Dante

1267–69 Thomas at the court of Clement IV at Viterbo. *On the Governance of Princes* and the *Commentary on Jeremias* (1267–69)

1268 Beheading of Konradin, the last Hohenstaufen, at Naples

1269–72 Thomas again at the University of Paris. *De Malo* (after 1269). *On the Virtues* (1269–72). *Commentaries on Aristotle and the Gospel of St John* (1269–72). *Commentary on the Pauline Epistles* (1269–73). *Compendium of Theology* (1272–73).

1270 Death of King Louis IX of France

1272 Thomas goes to Naples

1273 Election of the Emperor Rudolf of Hapsburg

1274 Death of St. Thomas Aquinas at Fossanova (March 7)

1280 Death of St. Albertus Magnus

1321 Death of Dante

1323 Canonization of St. Thomas Aquinas

1567 Thomas is made a Doctor of the Church

NOTES

I

Although it is not the point of this essay to be historical, it goes without saying that this sketch of St.
Thomas claims to be verifiable on historical evidence
—not only on questions of detail but also concerning
the total appreciation. It would seem incongruous,
however, to burden this short introductory presenta-
tion with a wealth of citations and references. In-
formed readers will easily notice how heavily the
author is indebted, particularly in the realm of historical facts, to the research of Denifle, Ehrle, Grabmann,
Mandonnet, Seppelt, and others. I should add that
historians vary in their interpretations of certain biographical details (as, f.i., the exact date of St. Thomas's
sojourn in Cologne). I refer for this to the works of
Angelus Walz, O.P.

1   Ernst Kantorowicz, *Kaiser Friedrich II*, vol. I,
    (Berlin, 1927), pp. 124ff.
2   This refusal of St. Thomas, which some may
    consider as customary among that first generation
    of mendicants, was in no way customary, but
    rather rested on an entirely personal decision. We
    know that Albertus Magnus became Bishop of

Regensburg in 1260. And one of St. Thomas's confrères, who had taught with him at Paris, Peter of Tarentaise, was made a cardinal and ultimately pope (Innocent V).

3 O. Tallgren, *Les Poésies de Rinaldo d'Aquino.* Mémoires de la Société Néophilologique de Helsingfors, vol. VI (1917), pp. 174-303.

4 I have discussed this relation more thoroughly in my book, *Fortitude and Temperance,* (Pantheon Books, New York, 1955), pp. 62ff.

5 *Commentaria in Job,* cap. 13, lect. 2.

6 *Commentaria in Metaphysicam Aristotelis,* lib. II, lect. 1.

7 *Commentaria in Dionysii (Pseudo-Areopagitae) De Divinis Nominibus,* cap. 4, lect. 4.

8 *Summa Theologica,* I, 2 prologue.

9 *De duobus praeceptis caritatis et decem legis praeceptis.*

10 "Our natural knowledge begins from sense. Hence our natural knowledge can go as far as it can be led by sensible things." *Summa Theologica,* I, 12, 12. "Although through Revelation we can become capable of knowing things which we otherwise would not know, we do not know them in any other way than through the senses." *Commentaria in librum Boethii De Trinitate,* 6, 3.

11 "It is clear that man is not just a soul, but something composed of body and soul." *Summa Theologica,* I, 75, 4.

12 *Summa Theologica,* II, II, 9, 4.

13 "All creatures are nothing but the real expression and reproduction of the types contained in the concept of the divine Word. For which reason all things are said to have been made by Him. It was fitting, therefore, that the Word should be united to a creature, namely human nature." *Summa Contra Gentiles*, IV, 42.

14 Cap. 1, lect. 5.

15 I, II, 38, 5.

16 *Quaestiones Disputatae de Veritate*, 2, 2.

17 *Commentaria in Evangelium S. Joannis*, cap. 1, lect. 7.

18 Among the errors of Averroism condemned by the Bishop of Paris in the year 1277 were the following: "There is no higher way of life than to keep oneself free (*vacare*) for philosophy." It seems to be a direct reply when Thomas writes in the *Summa Contra Gentiles* (III, 130): "The highest perfection of human life is that man's mind be occupied (*vacet*) with God."

19 *Commentaria in Epistolam S. Pauli Apostoli ad Colossenses*, cap. 2 lect. 1.

20 *Summa Theologica*, I, II, 113, 9 ad 2.

21 Siger de Brabantia, *Quaestiones de anima intellectiva*, 7.

22 *Commentaria in Aristotelis De Caelo et mundo*, I, 22.

23 So in the Encyclical *Studiorum Decem* of June 29, 1923. We quote: "May the instruction of Canon Law be held sacred by all: 'Professors are

obliged to form their philosophical and theological studies and the teaching of these subjects according to the method, the teaching and the basic principles of the Doctor Angelicus; and further, they are to revere the same.' Each one should observe this law in such a way that he is able to call St. Thomas his master." "Can anything express more clearly the high opinion of the Church for this Doctor, than the fact that the Tridentine Fathers determined that during all of their sessions only two books should be reverently placed before them on the altar, namely, the Holy Scriptures and the *Summa Theologica*."—On the other hand, the Encyclical warns against a pedantic and unfruitful canonization of St. Thomas, which would be contradictory to his own spirit: "Individuals shall not require more from each other than the Church, the Teaching Mistress and Mother of all, requires from all. In such questions, in which among esteemed Catholic authors different opinions confront each other with equal right, no one shall be hindered from following the view which seems to him to contain more truth."

24 *Summa Contra Gentiles*, II, 3.
25 Compare the concept of reason presented in J. Pieper, *Fortitude and Temperance*, pp. 57ff.
26 I, 3, prologue.
27 *Quaestiones Disputatae de Potentia Dei*, 7, 5, ad 14.

This essay contains the revised text of an article which originally appeared in the review, *Dieu Vivant* (20: Paris, 1951), with the title, *De l'élément négatif dans la philosophie de Saint Thomas d'Aquin*. It was published in a condensed form in the periodical *Hochland* (Munich, 1953).

The short quotation at the beginning of this essay is taken from the *Tao Té Ching* of Lao-tse (part 1, chapter 1).

1 Martin Heidegger, *Platons Lehre von der Wahrheit* (Berne, 1947), p. 5.

2 This is clearly brought out in Karl Eschweiler's book *Die zwei Wege der neueren Theologie* (Augsburg, 1926), pp. 81ff., 283, 296. Other theses which he proposes are more open to debate.

3 Cf. Josef Pieper, *Wahrheit der Dinge*, 2nd edition (Munich, 1951).

4 The paragraph in question is no. 12, which discusses "the famous scholastic sentence: *omne ens est unum—verum—bonum*."

5 Romano Guardini, *Welt und Person* (Würzburg, 1940), p. 110.

6 Jean-Paul Sartre, *L'existentialisme est un humanisme* (Paris, 1946), p. 94.

7 Sartre, op. cit., p. 22.

8 *Summa Theologica*, I, 93, 6.

9 *Quaestiones Disputatae de Veritate*, 1, 2.

10 I Timothy, vi, 4.

11 Commentary on the *Liber de Causis*, I, 6.

12 *L'existentialisme*, pp. 20ff., pp. 73ff.

13 *Summa Theologica*, I, 21, 2.

14 *Summa Theologica*, I, 16, 2.

15 *Quaestiones Disputatae de Veritate*, I, 1.

16 *Confessions*, XIII, 38. Cf. also *De Trinitate*, VI, .10.

17 Commentary *in Joannem*, I, 2.

18 *Summa Theologica*, I, 14, 12 ad 3.

19 Thomas quotes this sentence for instance in *Summa Theologica*, I, 16, 1; *Summa Contra Gentiles*, I, 60; *Quaestiones Disputatae de Veritate*, I, 2.

20 *Quia de Deo scire non possumus quid sit, sed quid non sit, non possumus considerare de Deo quomod sit, sed potius quomodo non sit.* (*Summa Theologica*, I, 3, prologue.)

21 I, 2 ad 1.

22 *Quaestio Disputata de Potentia Dei*, 7, 5 ad 14.

23 In the first chapter.

24 Commentary *in Aristotelem, De anima*, I, 1, 15.

25 *Quaestio Disputata de Spiritualibus Creaturis*, 11 ad 3.

26 *Quaestiones Disputatae de Veritate*, 4, 1 ad 8.

27 *Ibid.*

28 *Quaestiones Disputatae de Veritate*, 5, 2 ad 11.

29 *Summa Theologica*, I, 15, 2.

30 *Quaestiones Disputatae de Veritate*, 18, 2 ad 5.

31 *Summa Theologica*, I, II, 31, 5.

32 *Apologia doctae ignorantiae*, 2, 20ff.

33 *Metaphysics*, II, I, ('993b).

34 Commentary *in Metaphysicam Aristotelis*, II, I, no. 286.

III

This essay is a slightly altered version of a lecture delivered by the author in the Ateneo at Madrid and Barcelona. It appeared under the title of *Actualidad del Tomismo* in the collection "O Crece o Muere," a series edited by Florentino Perez Embid (Madrid, 1952).

1 The subject was thus formulated by the organizers of the lecture series, in which this conference was originally given.

2 *Quaestiones Disputatae de Spiritualibus Creaturis*, 10 ad 8.

3 *L'existentialisme*, p. 22.

4 Commentary *in Aristotelem de Anima*, I, 1, no. 15.

5 *Metaphysics*, VII, I, (1028b).

6 Commentary *in Metaphysicam Aristotelis*, I, 3, no. 64.

7 Friedrich Engels, *Ludwig Feuerbach und der Ausgang der klassischen deutschen Philosophie* (Berlin, 1946), pp. 17ff.

8 This sentence from Engels is quoted, for instance, in the official history of the Communist Party in the Soviet Union, *Geschichte der Kommunisti-*

schen Partei der Sowjetunion (Berlin, 1946), pp. 136f., in the section on dialectical and historical materialism authored by Stalin. According to I. M. Bochenski on Soviet-Russian dialectical materialism, in *Der sowjetrussische dialektische Materialismus* (Berne and Munich, 1950), p. 95, the Philosophical Institute of the Soviet Academy of Sciences devoted a full paragraph to Engels' proposition, which is quoted also by Lenin. This reference occurs in the Institute's 1948 edition of the *Program for an Extensive Course in Dialectical and Historical Materialism.*

9 *"L'homme se fait; il n'est pas tout fait d'abord, il se fait en choisissant sa morale." L'existentialisme,* p. 78.

10 *L'existentialisme,* p. 20.

11 Commentary on the *Epistle to the Colossians,* I, 4.

12 This same expression "in place of the Ideas" is used in another passage to denote the position of St. Augustine. "Augustine, following Plato, in so far as this was compatible with Catholic belief, did not accept self-subsistent original patterns of things: in their place *(loco earum)* he assumed that the original patterns of things existed in God." Cf. Quaest. Disp. de Spir. Creat. 10 ad 8.

13 *De Trinitate,* vi, 10.

14 *L'existentialisme,* p. 22.

15 Canon 1366, section 2, of the *Codex Juris Canonici,* makes the teaching of St. Thomas obliga-

tory for the philosophical and theological training of clerical students. It speaks not only of the doctrine and principles but also of the method of St. Thomas.

16 Reference may be made here to an article by Father John Baptist Lotz, S.J., in *Scholastik* for 1952 (no. 27), with the title *Von der Geschichtlichkeit der Wahrheit.* His argument is the following: "On one side, man strives after truth . . . but on the other, for the very sake of the truth, he must *realize* his truth . . . for only in this way will truth really come into his possession and be experienced as truth in important regions of experience" (p. 503).

Postscript

1 *Ea autem scientia, quae propter se tantum quaeritur, homo non potest libere uti . . . nec etiam ad nutum subest homini, cum ad eam perfecte homo pervenire non possit. Illud tamen modicum, quod ex ea habetur, praepronderat omnibus, quae per alias scientias cognoscuntur.* Commentary *in Metaphysicam Aristotelis,* I, 3, no. 60.

DATE DUE

JE 5 '68			
JE 5 '66			
RESERVE			
RESERVE MAR 3 1 1999			
MAR 3 1 1999			
GAYLORD			PRINTED IN U.S.A.

Printed in the USA
CPSIA information can be obtained
at www.ICGtesting.com
LVHW051939291124
797892LV00001B/160